Robert Orrell was born in Manchester in 1934. He joined the RAF Mountain Rescue Service at the age of 18, leaving after four hours to become a lighthouse keeper in the Outer Hebrides. Later he joined the Forestry Commission, and then the staff of Brathay Hall Outdoor Centre in the Lake District, transferring to a Merchant Navy school as an instructor in seamanship. He has been a teacher at an Outward Bound school, and has run his own sailing and climbing school, and served as a mountain guide.

He worked for a spell as a yacht delivery skipper in the Mediterranean, and then as a radio operator on a North Sea oil rig. When the rig blew up he took up lobster fishing, then served as second mate on a coaster. Several attempts to establish himself in business have led to shortage of money, which on each occasion has sent him back to wage-earning. The collapse of one such attempt led indirectly to the journey recounted in this book.

Mr Orrell has written several articles on mountaineering and the countryside and is a regular contributor to local newspapers and radio.

D0795119

Robert Orrell

Saddle Tramp in the Lake District

A MAYFLOWER BOOK

GRANADA
London Toronto Sydney New York

Published by Granada Publishing Limited in 1982

ISBN 0 583 13545 5

First published in Great Britain by
Robert Hale Limited 1979
Copyright © Robert Orrell 1979

Granada Publishing Limited
Frogmore, St Albans, Herts AL2 2NF
and
36 Golden Square, London W1R 4AH
366 United Nations Plaza, New York, NY 10017, USA
117 York Street, Sydney, NSW 2000, Australia
100 Skyway Avenue, Rexdale, Ontario, M9W 3A6, Canada
61 Beach Road, Auckland, New Zealand

Printed and bound in Great Britain
by Cox and Wyman Ltd, Reading
Set in Times

Granada ®
Granada Publishing ®

Contents

	Acknowledgements	9
1	Plans and Preparations	13
2	Pack-Saddle Problems	29
3	Two Steps Forward, One Step Back	39
4	Gillerthwaite to Gatesgarth	49
5	Unfriendly Watendlath	58
6	Over Sticks Pass to Patterdale	68
7	Martindale	85
8	Along High Street	94
9	Delay in Kentmere	101
10	Round Trip to Haweswater	116
11	Hagg End Farm	125
12	Brathay	135
13	Onwards into Dunnerdale	148
14	Near Tragedy in Mosedale	157
15	Brotherilkeld to Brantrake	167
16	The Last Leg	174

To my wife, Pauline,
for making it possible

Illustrations

The author making his pack-saddle
Jewel carrying the completed saddle
The ponies after the return trip over Black Sail Pass
Thor enjoying a roll in the grass
Crossing the Ford at Gatesgarth, Buttermere
Weatherbound at Gatesgarth
Pack-saddle problems on Sticks Pass
Stranded Jeep on Garburn Pass
Peggy Crossland
Jewel sinks into a bog
Campsite overlooking Ullswater
Pillar Rock from Gillerthwaite
Never-ending chore of mending tack
The journey over

MAP

All photographs taken by the author

Acknowledgements

To name everyone who was kind and helpful to me during my journey would fill another book, yet, in addition to those mentioned in the text, I must single out the following for their special assistance – Dave Barras; Roger Boothroyd, for providing me with a new anorak; Alf Davies, for the loan of photographic equipment; and Sue Cheesbrough, for the many laborious hours spent checking and typing the manuscript.

R.O.

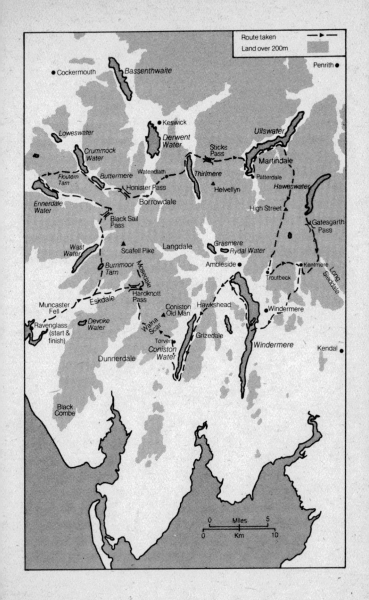

CHAPTER 1

Plans and Preparations

The ponies snorted with relief as they reached the final crest of the drove road, winding relentlessly up Muncaster Fell from the ancient port of Ravenglass. Turning in the saddle I looked back along the way we had come. It was early evening in May, but the crow-black clouds of an approaching storm had devoured the sun and plunged the countryside into a sombre gloom. Far below, the grey Irish Sea rolled listlessly along the Cumberland coast, awaiting the command of the wind god, to rise hissing with fury and grind the defenceless shingle beach into sand. Tiny finches twittered anxiously among the branches of unconcerned conifers and wise old cows bellowed a warning as they retreated downhill to shelter in the lea of the wood. An icy blast of wind sent a shiver through me as it bit into my anorak and I felt utterly miserable. I was forty-two years of age, on the verge of bankruptcy, besieged by creditors, a failure at everything I had attempted and now leaving my family to fend for themselves while I took off on horseback to satisfy an obscure ambition.

It seemed that so enraged were the gods at my selfishness that they were turning the elements against me, but, as a sudden vicious rain shower was hurled at my anorak hood, it made me all the more determined to see it through and driving my heels hard into Thor's flanks, I shot forward towards the darkening fells, towing a reluctant Jewel behind me.

I suppose everyone has a secret dream of some sort, which helps to make life bearable as they gaze longingly out of a window in one of those perpendicular greenhouses called office blocks, or while monotonously fitting this bit to that in a computerized, unionized, dehumanized hell-hole of a factory. Basically, the majority of us are optimists. We must be, otherwise we could not cope with the turmoil and problems of life, but fulfilling a dream or realizing an ambition is not easy while we have to struggle to make ends meet, and a man with a family has to think hard before punching his boss on the nose and rushing off to sail his Mirror-class dinghy round Cape Horn.

I have never been one of those people who could settle to what my father called a 'decent and respectable job', but in an attempt to put down roots for the benefit of my family I set up a small woodworking business in the picturesque village of Ravenglass, where the Rivers Esk, Irt and Mite join together in a natural harbour among the sand dunes of the Cumberland coast. The village was founded by the Romans in the dim and distant past, seventy-nine years before the wrath of the authorities in Jerusalem caused a young carpenter to be put to death and the calendars changed from BC to AD. Though the talented Italians were clever with wood and attempted to establish trade with the native Cumbrians they met with little success and never really prospered. When I arrived, two thousand years later, I discovered that the situation had not changed very much. Not being a joiner by trade, I concentrated my efforts on making gates, feed-troughs and a multitude of other bits and pieces for the agricultural community, but it was a wearying existence. Being the world's worst businessman I made the mistake, right from the start, of not charging enough and, although I got plenty of orders, I never made enough profit to pay my way and a flow of irate letters from my bank manager began to clog up my letter-box.

Farmers are notoriously slow at paying their bills and many a time I reached my bank with only minutes to spare before the manager refused to honour a cheque I had sent to a timber supplier. Driving round farms to collect my money was a waste of time. They would see me coming up the lane and by the time I drove into the yard the only sign of life would be a few hens picking at bits of corn or a dog snarling through a hole in a rotting outhouse door. I tried a dozen different ruses to get one cunning old devil to pay up, but he was always one jump ahead of me. Finally, I got so exasperated, I went to his farm one night and lit a fire in his field. He rushed out of the house, thinking his haystack was ablaze, and I nabbed him. I got my money, and a glass of whisky.

I battled on, but it soon became obvious that time was running out for my ailing enterprise. Every post brought gloom and doom and I went cold if the telephone rang or there was a knock on the door. I lived in a constant state of nervous tension, existing on a diet of tranquillizers, headache pills and stomach medicine, having frequent bitter rows with my wife, and rapidly becoming a physical and mental wreck. It could not go on, and it was not long before I was sitting in the waiting-room of a Whitehaven solicitor, clutching a cardboard file containing a wad of letters, all commencing, 'Unless we receive payment' and a statement from the Midland Bank, so red it might have been written with my own blood. The list of creditors was endless and the number of assets pitiful, so the solicitor decided the only course of action was a letter to everyone who was owed money, explaining the situation.

The one thing which kept me sane through the months of strain and worry was a dream that had helped me over many difficult times during my life. I had promised myself that one day I would get a pony and explore the ancient drovers' roads and pack-horse routes that criss-crossed the high fells of the Lake District. To carry my gear I would take a pack-pony and wander as I wished, free to pitch my tent by a clear mountain beck and watch the subtle colours of the fells blend into the night. It was a lovely dream, but as the years rolled by and I staggered from one financial crisis to another, the chances of it being fulfilled got slimmer with every bank statement.

A week after my visit to the solicitor I started to sell off the woodworking machines I had, together with my stock of timber. It was a depressisng business and, one day, unable to endure it any longer, I bought a ticket on the Ravenglass and Eskdale Railway and, leaving the train at Irton Road Station, I made my way up Mitredale. Somehow, even at the height of summer, when visitors swarm over the fells in their thousands, you can find peace in Mitredale. It was a lovely, crisp day, with just a whisper of wind showering the valley with a mingled perfume of spruce and bracken. I sat with my back against an old oak and, lulled by the rippling of the quiet river, I fell into a deep sleep. When I awoke the huge golden orb of the evening sun floated on a thin wisp of cotton-wool cloud, ready to sink swiftly into the Irish Sea and bring down the curtain on another day. I was stiff and cold, but felt so fit and relaxed I was able to think clearly for the first time in months. It was a marvellous feeling and my head buzzed with excitement as I stumbled over Muncaster Fell in the dark, towards Ravenglass. There was more to life than worrying myself into an early grave just because I owed a few pounds here and there. Instead of dreaming about it, I was free to saddle my pony, load a tent and food on to a pack-pony and wander the fells wherever the paths led me. There were just one or two snags. I did not own a saddle or ponies, and food cost money. By the time the lights of the village came into view excitement had given way to despair.

'If you don't go now, you never will do,' said my wife, banging a lump of dough on the table and sending up a cloud of flour that descended like a mantle of snow over the dog, fast asleep in front of the kitchen fire. He was too occupied, growling at a dreamland cat to notice. 'I'll get a job,' she went on, 'and we'll manage all right until you get back. I've got sixty pounds in the bank and you can have that to see you through.'

I had put the idea to her apprehensively, not quite knowing how she would react to me disappearing into the fells for several weeks, leaving the family without any financial support. Realizing how much the journey meant to me, she had characteristically found a way round the obstacles. All I had to do now was to find ponies and equipment and I could be away.

A search through the attic unearthed my long neglected tent, sleeping-bag and camping gear. I scrounged an old army saddle off a farmer I knew. It had been lying in a barn for years and was green with mould.

'Aye,' said Charlie, looking at the saddle wistfully, 'it's been lying yonder many a year. 'Twas our John as allus used it.'

John must have been a hell of a queer shape. The right stirrup was six inches wide, while the left was less than three. Getting a saddle was one thing, but finding a horse to attach it to, plus another to carry my gear, was not going to be easy. They needed to be tough native ponies, used to mountain country and capable of living off what they could find. I had no money for fancy feeds, or room to carry any.

Thor came into my life quite by chance. I happened to visit a farm near Broughton in Furness, and, while walking across the fields with Helen Woodhouse, the owner, a hefty black Fell pony kept shoving his face into our pockets, looking for titbits. Standing about fourteen hands high, with enormous shoulders and quarters, he was everything a working Fell pony should be. I was thinking aloud when I blurted out, 'I wish I could borrow a grand animal like him for a couple of months.' Helen never batted an eyelid. 'Well take him then, the exercise will do him good.' He was to prove a good friend and, despite having picked up a few bad habits in his sixteen years, a gentle temperament made up for his faults. Of his two speeds, slow and stop, he preferred the latter, but helped along by a vigorous heel, he would go all day.

It was now March and, though I planned to leave at the beginning of May, I was having great difficulty in finding a suitable pony to carry the pack. I scoured the whole of Cumbria, but people would either promise to lend me a pony then change their minds, or I would find it was so ancient that it could hardly carry itself, let alone a pack-saddle. April approached and I was becoming desperate. Not only could I not find a pack-pony, the genuine pack-saddle seemed to have vanished into antiquity. Advertisements in horsy magazines brought no response and a reply from the Army Royal Corps of Transport regretted that their remaining stock of pack-saddles had recently been disposed of in Hong Kong.

'Alan Ellwood's got a couple of Fell ponies over in Dunnerdale,' growled the old sage from behind a pint of Guinness. I was in the back bar of the Pennington Arms in Ravenglass, pouring ale into a local horse-dealer, hoping to find out if he knew of anyone who would lend me a good Fell pony. Cumberland horse-dealers suffer from a type of amnesia which demands liberal quantities of booze before the condition is relieved, and the crafty old codger was about to start his seventh pint at my expense when he forgot himself and let slip the information about ponies in Dunnerdale.

On the phone next day Alan said yes, he would lend me a pony, but she had not been used for two years and was a bit frisky. When we arrived to collect her, Jewel was not just frisky, she was positively murderous and it took a lot of heaving and dodging of flailing hooves and bared teeth before she was fastened in the box for the journey to

Ravenglass. I had borrowed a brand new horse-box and Jewel removed all the varnish off the inside more efficiently than any paint stripper. In the paddock at the back of my house, she shot out of the horse box like a brown bullet and for two days I could not get near her.

My daughter, Allison, eventually managed to tempt her with a bucket of feed and, slipping a halter over her head, brought her into the yard. What a sorry sight she looked. Her thick winter coat was caked hard with mud and she was pitifully thin. Though a registered Fell pony, she was a lot lighter in build than Thor and slightly smaller. My heart sank at the thought of trying to train this bedraggled heap of untamed horseflesh to carry a pack and behave safely on steep mountain paths. She made it quite plain she was not prepared to co-operate and any attempt to put a saddle on her back was met with fierce resistance. Allison worked hard on her everyday after school, but it looked as if she would never be ready in time. The mere sight of a saddle or bridle sent her into a fit of frenzied bucking and rearing. After days of solid perseverance Allison managed to get on Jewel's back and ride gently round the field.

'Look,' she shouted, 'I'm on her. I'll beat you to the gate.'

She beat me to the gate all right, but she was not on Jewel. The cunning little monster had taken advantage of Allison's brief lack of concentration and catapulted her over my head. Picking herself out of the mud she muttered a few words that little girls really should not use and hauling herself back into the saddle drove the reluctant Jewel round and round the field, over low jumps and cavaletti, until she was drooping at the knees. We never had any trouble catching her or tacking up after that.

To be well on my way before the tourist season started, I planned to leave on Sunday, 16 May, but with only three weeks to go I still had not tracked down a pack-saddle. With only £60 to my name it seemed pointless asking a saddler for a quotation, but curiosity got the better of me and I telephoned a firm well known in the Lake District.

'I wanted a pack-saddle similar to those used by the Army.'

'Aye, I know the one you mean,' said the voice on the other end of the phone, 'don't see many about these days.'

'How much do you reckon it would cost to make one?' I enquired.

'Well now, it's difficult to say, off hand. Let's see,' the voice died away to a murmur as he very likely pencilled some rapid calculations on the back of a cigarette packet. 'With breeching and breast strap,' the voice boomed back, 'I could let you have a pack-saddle for four hundred and fifty pounds, plus ten quid if you want a leather girth. There'll be VAT on top of that, mind.' The seconds ticked away. 'Hullo, are you still there?' the voice demanded. Yes, I was still there, it was just that I was having trouble getting my breath. How nice it must be to be able to say, £450, is that all? Can you let me have it by next week. Such are the fantasies of the poor.

There was only one way I was going to get a pack-saddle and that was to make one. I scoured books and magazines looking for a photograph of a pack-pony or mule, but the saddle was always hidden beneath sacks of grain being transported over the Andes, or the wheels and barrel of a field-gun on its way to quell an uprising on the Khyber Pass. Salvation came in the form of the local blacksmith, an ex-Army man, he had a copy of the *Manual of Horsemastership, Equitation and Animal Transport, 1937*. A marvellous publication, regrettably long out of print, it is a mine of information, whether your steed be a horse, mule, camel, bullock or elephant. The many photographs of pack-saddles gave me all the information I needed to make one and fit it correctly. My pack-saddle was not as smart as the army version, but with a few pieces of leather, canvas and foam rubber it is amazing what can be done. A friend who was a fitter in a local factory made the metal swivels out of stainless steel and the breeching and breast strap were made from bits of old cart harness I found in a derelict barn. The leather was so hard I had to soak it for weeks in leather oil before it would bend. Stitching it was agony.

Time whizzed by and with only a week to go to my departure date a lot of work still needed to be done on the pack-saddle. Girths had to be made from a roll of supple leather, given to me by a kindly soul, and a crupper and breast strap were needed for Thor's saddle. While I stitched furiously, a helpful neighbour, June Morris, exercised Thor every morning, towing Jewel behind on a lead rope. In the afternoons I spent an hour in a flat field familiarizing them with the hobbles I had made. These consisted of two lengths of heavy leather strap which buckled round the front fetlocks and were joined together by a short length of nylon rope. I was to discover later, to my cost, that light chain is preferable to nylon rope. The purpose of the hobble is to restrict a pony's movement and so prevent him from straying when one is camping in open country. At first Jewel tried to jump out of hers and promptly fell in a struggling heap. After a few more attempts at bolting, she got the hang of it and was soon grazing easily, moving each leg only a few inches, as she moved forward. Thor stared for a long time at the strange thing attached to his legs, but refused to budge. I tried to push him forward, but instead of moving he slowly crumpled at the knees and lay down. Having got him on his feet and hobbled again, I wafted an apple in front of his nose and in no time he was waddling round the field. It was a week or two before they were completely happy with the hobbles, but training them not to move too much when something was wrapped round their legs was to prove invaluable during the journey. After school my daughters, Allison and Joanne, rode the ponies along the soft sand of the beach to harden their muscles.

With two days to go, Jewel ripped the breeching to pieces. She had behaved perfectly as I fitted the saddle on her back, even when I pulled the unfamiliar crupper strap under her tail, she did not seem too offended, but a sudden gust of wind flapped one of the canvas carriers as it hung from the saddle and Jewel exploded. She reared up, dragging the lead rope out of Allison's hands and, before I could grab her, was away down the yard as though the devil himself was after her. The field gate was open a foot or two and as she barged through it the breeching straps got caught up. Something had to give, and I watched, helpless, as hours of laborious stitching were torn apart and strips of leather fluttered about the field like confetti. It took most of that night to make a new breeching and, bog-eyed and irritable, I banged the saddle on Jewel's back the next morning, making it very clear I was in no mood for her antics. She got the message and gave no trouble as various adjustments were made to straps and buckles. By early afternoon all was ready for a trial run with the packs. The Army manual illustrated a number of ingenious ways of attaching a load to a pack-saddle, but most of them appeared to require the assistance of a burly sergeant. I needed a foolproof system for packing my gear quickly each day and attaching it to the saddle, without having to hang on to the load with one hand, feverishly trying to tie knots with the other, while the impatient Jewel moved off to investigate a new patch of grass. The simplest method seemed to be an ex-Army kit-bag slung on either side of the saddle, containing my food, clothes, sleeping-bag etc, with a third, containing the tent, placed across the top. The side bags were held in place by a wide canvas sling with strips of wood riveted to each end, one to fix the canvas to the saddle and the other, drilled with a series of holes, to take the lashing rope. It was an easy job to hold the kit-bag against the saddle, pull the canvas sling round it and tie it firmly to the steel swivels. It was crude, but it worked, and on the numerous occasions during my journey, when the pack slipped and I had to unload in a hurry, it never caused me any problems.

Jewel rolled her eyes at the sight of the packs and broke into a four-footed ballet dance, but with her nose in a bucket of feed she soon forgot about me and I was able to lash the three bags to the saddle before she realized what was happening. To get her used to the idea of the pack swaying behind her head, the bags were only stuffed with paper. It proved a wise precaution. On the way out of the yard one of the bags rubbed against the wall with a loud rasping noise and Jewel bolted. Allison hung on bravely, but was being dragged along the road. I shouted to her to let go and, free of the drag, the exasperating brute disappeared at full speed on to the beach. When we found her she was standing up to her knee-caps in a hayfield, chewing steadily, like a placid Jersey cow. The saddle was still intact, but the bags had been torn in several places by a hawthorn hedge. Back in the village street, we warily steered clear of cars and lamp-posts and walked Jewel up and down until she became accustomed to the feel of the pack. Thor was quickly tacked up and, with Jewel in tow, looking as if she had carried a pack all her life, we rode on our first trip together, along the beach to Eskmeals. All the worry and strain of the last few weeks flowed away from me as the ponies lumbered slowly over the shingle and squelched through the mussel beds of the Esk estuary and I could not wait to set off on the real thing.

Saturday, 15 May, was an incredibly busy day. The blacksmith, having been promising to come every day for a week, turned up while we were having breakfast. Thor stood quite unconcerned while the smith hammered away at his big feet, but the look on Jewel's face gave a hint of impending disaster, so, leaving the children to hold innocently onto her halter rope, I made an excuse about having other things to do and fled into the house. The hammering started again and, any moment, I felt sure the blacksmith would come hurtling through the window, followed by his anvil, but nothing happened and later the sound of the blacksmith's van driving out of the yard announced that the job was finished. The cantankerous little devil had not flinched a muscle.

The list of food and equipment seemed endless and, as each item was ticked off the heap on the floor began to look as if it would take a string of pack-ponies to carry it, not just one. Jake Kelly and a film crew from BBC television news arrived as I was trying to decide what non-essentials could be left behind. They had to film somewhere else on Sunday and would I mind dressing up in my gear and 'leaving' now, so they could film it. I still had not had the chance to pack all my equipment into the kit-bags and try them out on the saddle, and, not wanting to risk the ignominy of the whole lot falling off while I was being filmed, I got the children to stuff the bags with paper. I rode down the street a couple of times and then was interviewed by Jake. It is always difficult explaining one's ambitions. To merely say 'because I want to' in reply to the question 'Why are you doing this?' is not dramatic enough for journalists, and they probe in hope of discovering a deeper emotional reason reaching back to the days when your great-great grandfather seduced the squire's daughter and they eloped to Gretna Green on the back of a donkey. The urge to ride having remained in the family ever since.

I did not see the television interview, but that night Radio Carlisle news announced that I was leaving on Sunday on a 200-mile journey on horseback, round the Lake District. I hoped my creditors were not listening. I worked deep into Saturday night, frantically trying to do a thousand last-minute jobs. The kit-bags were filled and emptied a dozen times before a place was found for everything, but the weight was frightening. I had a small spring balance in my kit to weigh the bags each day, to make sure the load was evenly distributed. The two side bags weighed eighty pounds apiece and the tent bag thirty pounds; it was far too heavy for little Jewel to carry over steep, rough ground and bog. Everything was dumped on the kitchen floor again and, after drastic weeding, the weight was reduced to a hundred and thirty pounds. It was too late to try it out on Jewel, and in any case I could hardly keep my eyes open.

I seemed to have only slept for five minutes when the jangling of the alarm-clock bell hammered its way into my numbed brain. My watch said 6 a.m. and I wondered why that irritating instrument was disturbing me at such an unearthly hour. I lay back for a few minutes to gather my senses and then the awful truth hit me. This was it. The day I had waited for during the many long years. The dream fulfilled, the ambition come true. I felt sick with apprehension. I could not face breakfast and went out into a grey murky morning to the stables. Allison and Joanne were up by the time I got back with the ponies, and set about giving them an extra special grooming. Thor was tacked up with the Army saddle on a multi-coloured blanket, and with a broad leather girth, crupper and breast strap, he looked very handsome. Jewel stood very patiently while all the paraphernalia of the pack-saddle was fastened round her, and then came the packs. They felt incredibly heavy, but were lashed into place and I was ready for a quick trial down the street. Hardly had I got out of the yard when the pack heeled over at a crazy angle. The girth was tightened a notch and we tried again. This time the pack fell right under Jewel's belly and everything had to be removed from her back. We tried all ways, but each time the pack slipped. Midday came and went and I was no nearer getting away. The girth was shortened and two blankets put under the saddle, but the effect was only marginal, the pack still fell over. To add to the difficulties it started pouring with rain in the afternoon, and within a short time we were wet, cold and thoroughly disheartened. In despair I emptied the contents of the kit-bags onto the kitchen floor to see what could be left behind. A lot of food was dumped and all my spare clothes except one change and a sweater. The weight was reduced to a little under a hundred pounds. Returning to the yard, I was relieved to find the rain had stopped and a pale sun was shining weakly through the clouds, but it was horribly cold. The pack slipped over the first time, but by carefully balancing the tent on top of the load I managed to go twice down the main street and everything stayed firm. It had gone eight o'clock when I finally got away. A great bank of black cloud was building up in the west and I was anxious to get well into Eskdale before dark. There was hardly a soul to be seen as the ponies plodded down the street and I waved good-bye to my wife and Joanne. Allison came with me on her pony for a little way, but at Muncaster Chase, where the Eskdale bridleway leaves the main road, she turned for home, and with a wave was gone. I was on my own. Far from being elated at the thought of setting out on a great adventure, I was tired and dejected. As I passed a house I could see a fire blazing in the hearth and I had a terrible longing to go home to mine. The path ahead was steep and as the ponies surged forward I made no move to stop them.

The heavy rain and the tall trees of Chapels Wood blotted out what little light remained and we descended through an inky blackness, slipping and slithering over a morass of mud and boulders, as the path dropped sharply down the fellside to High Eskholme. A cottage wall provided a bit of shelter from the gale as I fumbled in the pack for a torch. Everything had been stowed in such a rush I could not remember which bag I had put it in. Having tried, unsuccessfully, to switch on a rubbery object, I struck a match and found it was a banana. Another match uncovered the torch and I made a quick check of the pack and girths. Thankfully nothing had moved, but the ponies were an unhappy sight, their bodies plastered with slimy mud and broad rivulets of water streaming down their faces. Climbing back into the cold, wet saddle, it needed a few hefty digs into Thor's ribs before he lumbered forward into the night and a tight lead rope conveyed the message that Jewel was not exactly bursting with enthusiasm either, as she squelched in his wake.

The path wound along the base of the fell towards Muncaster Head and was broad and flat for most of its length. I flicked the torch on now and again, to make sure we were not going into a ditch, but I need not have bothered, the instinct of the ponies was enough to keep us on the path. After a while the wind dropped and the rain eased to a fine drizzle. A strong tang of soil, mingled with the perfume of rhododendrons, drifted out of the wood and I forgot I was cold and wet as I sucked in lungfuls of pure nectar.

The rain stopped altogether and the clouds melted away as the twinkling lights of Muncaster Head Farm came into view through the trees. Beyond the farm, the swollen River Esk foamed and thundered beneath the ponies' feet as we crossed the hump-backed bridge to the road at Forge House, and soon we were at Brantrake, where I planned to camp for the night. I was too tired to unpack everything, so I turned the ponies into a field and, leaving the tack where I had dropped it, pitched the tent. Calling at the house I was surprised to find David Sharp and his wife, Rachel, living there. For a number of years they had kept the delightful King George IV Inn, in Eskdale, and were well known to visitors for their friendly welcome. Having just sold the King George, they were waiting to move into a farm a little way down the valley. I sat for a while, yarning, but I was so weary I had to leave the pleasant company and crawl into the tent. Almost before the door flap had dropped behind me I was curled up and fast asleep.

CHAPTER 2

Pack-Saddle Problems

The morning was quiet and still when I awoke next day. I opened the tent door and lay back in my sleeping-bag to watch as the sun climbed over the top of Green Crag, bathing the valley in a blood-warming glow, as it mopped up the morning dew. As the sun's rays touched the resting sheep it brought them to life, and one by one they climbed stiffly to their feet to stand while toylike lambs eagerly sucked at their warm milk. It was a different world to the one I had left the night before and, as I stared out of the tent door at the peaceful valley, the problems of yesterday did not seem as important or as menacing. My wife had got a job, so at least the family could eat while I was away. None of my creditors were likely to die of starvation because I was temporarily leaping off the merry-go-round. Maybe the profit graph of the Midland Bank would plummet by a fraction of a millimetre, but there was no need for the directors to jump from the top floor of the Stock Exchange. I would be back, but meantime I would push the whole lot to the back of my mind and get on with enjoying my journey. It was as if the tension of a wound-up spring in my head was suddenly released and I felt great. Soon the breakfast bacon spluttered and sizzled on the primus stove and the aroma of coffee wafted up from the billy can. I was the happiest man on earth.

After breakfast I sorted out the chaos of the previous day's packing and made sure my spare clothes and sleeping-bag were well wrapped in polythene. Rain had seeped into the kit-bag, but luckily, apart from a label or two peeling off cans of food, there was no damage. I got away about 10 a.m., after spending an hour chasing David Sharp's labrador pup round the paddock, retrieving bits of gear she kept running off with. She thought it was a great game and no sooner had I prised a sock off her needle-sharp teeth and hastily stuffed it into a bag than she was off again dragging a sweater towards a gap in the fence. Swearing at her only increased the mischief, so I grabbed the squirming little horror by the scruff of the neck, shoved her into an outhouse and banged the door. I got on with my packing and was congratulating myself on having got rid of the pest when I felt a sharp nip on my ankle. There she was, grinning all over her face and wagging her tail like a mechanical carpet beater. I began to despair of ever finishing my packing when suddenly she grabbed a used coffee bag lying among some rubbish. As her teeth sank into the wet coffee grains the cheeky grin faded and a large 'Ugh!' took its place. The carpet-beating tail dropped to the ground and she slunk away to the gate, looked over her shoulder with an expression that had the unmistakable accusation, 'You did that on purpose'. I had not, but thanks to Messrs Lyons I finished my packing undisturbed.

At Forge Bridge we left the hard surface of the council's tarmacadam and followed the old drove road, meandering along the bank of the River Esk. Drooping birch trees, heavy with yesterday's rain, glistened in the bright sun and fat cows lay in the steaming grass, relaxing in Mother Nature's sauna bath. The ponies had rested well and needed no urging as we jogged steadily on, through meadow and gate, towards Dalegarth. Several times I had to leap off Thor and readjust the pack-saddle before it slid off Jewel's narrow back. I tried all sorts of ways of holding the saddle tight, but still the damned thing took on a list before we had gone very far.

Watching Jewel, I was sure the problem had a lot to do with the way she walked. She had a peculiar way of swinging her backside like a flirtatious dolly bird in tight jeans and it was the oscillations of those hairy hips that were playing havoc with my attempts to balance the load.

Beyond the farmland the path oozed through a tricky expanse of bog, then, swinging away from the river at Dalegarth Wood, it plunged under a canopy of towering conifers and oaks. Cut off from the sun, the chilly air beneath the trees was a reminder that summer was still some way off. A broad path wound purposefully through the silent wood, the surface pounded hard with the passage of countless thousands of men and animals. The Romans were the first to come this way, carrying supplies to their fort at Hardknott, then, as the country opened out and trade expanded, teams of pack-ponies carried wool from the dales' farms to the ports of West Cumberland, returning with food and all manner of goods. Cattle landed at Ravenglass from Scotland and the Isle of Man had their hooves shod with iron to protect them during the long, rough journey through the Esk valley and over the high passes to the markets of Kendal and beyond. There must have been some rich pickings for the bad lads of the day, as unguarded pack-horses passed through the woods, loaded with brandy, rum and tobacco.

The quaint round chimneys of Dalegarth Hall came into view as soon as we were out of the wood and I stopped to peer over the wall at the house, beautifully constructed of local granite and thought to be one of the oldest buildings in Eskdale.

Way back in the twelfth century it was called Austhwaite Hall, taking its name from Austhwaite estate, which stretched from Harter Fell, beside Hardknott Pass and enclosed a vast chunk of land on the south side of the River Esk, as far down as Linbeck Mill, out to Devoke Water and the wild expanse of Birker Moor. The tenants of the isolated farms scattered about the estate would have scratched a desperately miserable existence from the poor land and what few animals they possessed. At times they were close to starvation and the deer roaming about the woods must have been very tempting. For the seemingly trivial offence of bagging one for the pot the manorial lords dealt out rough justice and in the sixteenth century the occupier of a small farm called Scales, high on Birker Moor, was hanged for deer-stealing.

The de Austhwaite family owned their estate for over two hundred years, until Thomas de Austhwaite was unable to produce anything but girls and the male line became extinct about 1345. His daughter, Constance, married Nicholas Stanley of Greysouthen, near Cockermouth.

According to one historian, the name Dalegarth first appears in records about 1437, when Thomas Stanley, great-grandson of Nicholas, married Anne Hudleston. For years the experts have speculated and argued about the reason why Austhwaite became Dalegarth and whether the present hall is built on the site of the original. Could it be that the lord of the manor, not liking the crumbling heap of stones he had inherited, preferred to build a brand new house with all the mod cons of the day. Maybe he did not even like the name of the old dwelling and gave it a new one, much like the present day chap who acquires 'Chez Nous' and changes it to 'Dunroamin'.

Dalegarth Hall was the home of the Stanley family until sometime in the seventeenth century, when John Stanley built a hall at Ponsonby a few miles north of Gosforth. Much of the old hall at Dalegarth was pulled down during the mid eighteenth century and what remained was later renovated by Sir John Ramsden of Muncaster Castle, Ravenglass. In 1947, after an interval of some two hundred and fifty years, the Stanley family regained their ancestral home when Mr Nicholas Stanley acquired the estate from the Ramsdens of Muncaster.

* * *

I let the ponies snatch a few mouthfuls of grass while I juggled for the umpteenth time with the packs. Having checked Jewel carefully for any sign of the pack-saddle or harness chafing, we left the drove road and the sound of iron-shod hooves rang loud as we clattered along the surfaced road, over Trough House Bridge, to the main valley road by Dalegarth Railway Station. A number of cars passed on the narrow road and Jewel became very edgy and tried to bolt past Thor, almost dragging me out of the saddle. I had just managed to calm her down and was disentangling the lead from Thor's neck when a fast-approaching car sounded his horn loudly. Jewel reared up, pawing the air with her forelegs, and though I waved frantically at the car to get the driver to slow down, he continued sounding his horn as he drove past. Jewel's antics upset Thor and, with the pair of them careering about in the road, how that car missed us I will never know. Both the lunatic driver and his wife were laughing all over their stupid faces as they roared past and added further to their little joke by sticking a hand out of the car window, giving the sign, one version Winston Churchill was famous for, and the reverse made Harvey Smith notorious. To the half-wit driver of a new Rover 2000, with a Birmingham registration, my sincerest wish is that his shiny monster will break down on the summit of Hardknott Pass, late one Sunday night, while a lovely Lakeland rainstorm drums my greetings into the expensive paintwork of its roof.

The ponies were so jumpy I had to lead them along the rest of the way, through the tiny hamlet of Boot, to the foot of the path to Wasdale. The pack leaned at a crazy angle, but with more cars appearing my only thought was to get away from the road, and quick. Jewel has a way of forgetting cars, earthquakes and similar catastrophes when she spies something to eat, and, with her nose buried in the flower bed of a rather attractive cottage by Boot Mill, she soon stopped shaking. By heaving at the pack I managed to right it without having to go through the tedious business of removing the harness. The sound of a heavy bolt being flung back on the cottage door drew my attention to a row of headless daisies in the flower bed, and, urging Thor forward, I dragged the protesting Jewel after me, still chewing a mouthful of incriminating evidence. It was not necessary to be in earshot to know what the owner of the flower bed was shouting after us and I drove the ponies on at such a pace they were soaked with sweat by the time we reached the last gate leading on to the open fell.

Ahead the path climbed steadily up, through bog and boulders, towards the great sprawling mass of Scafell, and the ponies puffed and wheezed with the effort of learning to walk together. Normally the slope would have been no trouble to either of them, but being 'fastened' together disturbed their rhythm. Thor's mighty legs drove him forward at a faster pace than little Jewel's, and when the lead rope became taut she had to run to catch up. To prevent Jewel from ending up with a neck as long as a giraffe I had to hold Thor back, and at this uncomfortable, lurching gait we staggered upwards, towards Burnmoor Tarn. The lively movement disturbed the pack and, having swayed about all the way up, it slid off altogether, just as we reached the tarn, and hung under Jewel's belly in a tangle of rope and harness. There was plenty of time to reach Wasdale before dark, so I let the ponies graze while I got out the primus stove and made a brew of tea. I was not very hungry, but, discovering a vintage Mars Bar in my anorak pocket I lay back against a rock and spent an absorbing ten minutes removing numerous assorted nails, bits of straw, a couple of pony nuts and other foreign bodies embedded in the chocolate covering. It tasted no worse for having 'matured' for a month or two.

A sudden movement caught my eye from the direction of Wasdale and over a rocky hillock came a line of ponies. They probably belonged to a farm in the valley, but were moving so slowly, in single file, they could have been a funeral procession of a hundred years ago, for this was the old Corpse Road. In the days before Wasdale Head had its own consecrated ground, those unfortunate enough to expire in this remote corner of Cumberland were denied their final rest until the mortal remains had been carried, on horseback, for burial at St Catherine's in Eskdale. There are numerous tales told of horses bolting and disappearing into the mist, still carrying the coffin, never to be seen again, but the one I like best concerns a farmer in Wasdale who was plagued by a nagging wife. Blessed relief came one day, when the wife took ill and died. She was quickly put in a coffin and the funeral party set off for Eskdale. Crossing Burnmoor the pony slipped and the coffin bumped against a rowan tree and revived the old wife. There was nothing they could do but troop back to Wasdale, where she made the poor man's life even more miserable. After a few years she finally passed away, and once more the funeral party set off for Eskdale. The farmer was very careful not to jolt the coffin and, as they neared the rowan tree, he shouted to his son, who was leading the pony, 'Be careful as thou passes yon tree, Jack. We don't want any more accidents.'

Jewel was busy mowing a patch of grass and hardly noticed as I heaved on the pack-saddle girth and loaded the packs on top. Thor had tasted neither water nor grass, but stood deep in equine thought, staring at the western horizon. Perhaps there was an attractive filly we did not know about, or could it be a crafty idea forming in his horsy mind. I was to find out a couple of days later. Leaving Burnmoor Tarn the path was pleasant, firm turf, but as it descended towards Wasdale countless rainstorms had torn the surface away and gouged deep ravines through the slimy peat. The ponies skidded and tobogganed their way through a sea of rocks and mud with a display of footwork that would have left the Royal Ballet gasping with admiration, till, on the rim of Wasdale, we halted and gaped at one of the most fantastic views I have seen in a long time. The air was crystal clear and it was as if the whole valley had been magnified a million times. The surface of Wastwater was so still, Illgill Head and the vast stretch of screes below were mirrored in minute detail, like a giant, elongated photograph. Across the valley the long ridge of Yewbarrow stood out sharp as a razor against a pale blue sky, with every patch of bracken, buttress of rock and blade of grass so clearly visible it was uncanny. Among the tiny green fields on the valley floor, each neatly divided by rugged grey stone walls, stood Wasdale Head Chapel, built originally from ships' timbers, washed up on the Cumberland coast, its walls held together with burnt seaweed and shells. Where the old highways of Black Sail and Sty Head Pass merged together beneath the mass of Kirk Fell, the whitewashed buildings of the Wastwater Hotel shone like a beacon in the bright sunlight. Blocking the head of the valley, the great bulk of the king of English mountains, Scafell Pike, towered over his subjects at a superior 3,206 feet. Although the steep crags of Great Gable were the home of British rock-climbing, it was to Scafell Pike that the early tourists were drawn. The dalesfolk found a new source of income in the wealthy Victorians and for the princely sum of ten shillings the visitor could be conveyed, with a guide, from Wastwater Hotel to his lofty Mecca, on the back of a pony. Having the highest mountain, the smallest church and the deepest lake in England all in one valley, Wasdale was a tourist attraction long before some of the more fashionable Lakeland resorts sold their first ice-cream.

I was so lost in thought as I sat gazing at the view, I had not noticed a bank of black cloud creeping across the sun, and a sudden sharp shower sent me scampering for my anorak. It passed quickly and, having untangled Jewel's lead rope and hauled Thor away from a patch of grass, we set off down the steep track. The pack-saddle had behaved itself, despite the rough journey from Burnmoor Tarn, and full of confidence and well-being, I urged the ponies forward, eager to pitch my tent by the peaceful lake.

The path went through a narrow gate in a wall and, having wedged the gate open with a boulder, I tied Jewel's lead rope to my saddle and led Thor gently through the opening. Turning to help Jewel I realized, to my horror, that the pack was too wide to go through. I shouted to Thor to stop, but the big idiot took not the slightest bit of notice and, as the lead rope tightened, little Jewel was dragged forward and the pack stuck fast. She tried to rear up and with a roar like the ending of the world, the wall crashed down, sending chunks of stone bouncing in all directions. That should have been enough, but there was more to come. Both ponies bolted for their lives and, reaching a tree, Thor shot past on one side and Jewel on the other. Reasonable enough, you might think, except that they were still tied together. As the rope tightened there was a mighty crack and Thor sped on, minus the saddle. I stood rooted to the spot for a minute or two. In the saddle-bag, which hit the rocks with a sickening thud, were my camera lenses and binoculars. Fortunately they survived the impact and I was glad I had decided to carry them in polystyrene packing rather than a fancy leather case. My comfortable Army saddle looked a sorry mess. Both girth straps had snapped on one side and the seat was badly scoured by sharp rock. Thor's breast strap had also parted at the buckles. Having tied Jewel to a tree, I got out the mending gear and started the laborious job of sewing all the pieces together. I was in no mood to go chasing after Thor, and, while I forced thread through the tough leather, I could see him peering sheepishly from behind a large rock. An hour went by before I got the ponies and saddles together again and, leading them carefully, we reached the foot of the path by Brackenclose without further mishap.

At Wasdale Head Hall Farm I pitched the tent on an expanse of soft turf and, while the ponies rolled the sweat off their backs, I relaxed against a tree trunk with a mug of hot coffee and watched the evening sun turn the surface of the lake blood-red. The fresh smell of sheep mingled with the aroma of wet grass and there was not a sound, save the bleating of lambs and a hungry calf bellowing occasionally from a distant outbuilding. A pair of mallard ducks glided silently over the water, spreading a wide V wake across the still, flat surface.

Before the dying sun flung its last few darts at the fell tops, I rummaged through my meagre stock of food, trying to decide what to have for dinner. I tried my luck with a labelless tin and was rewarded with hamburgers and beans. Taking a last look out of the tent door, the sky seemed promising for the next day. The clouds had cleared and a sky full of stars gave a hope of settled weather. Wrapped in my down sleeping-bag I let the night look after itself.

CHAPTER 3

Two Steps Forward, One Step Back

The sound of torrential rain beating on the canvas woke me at 6 a.m. A peep out of the door revealed a wet, dismal world, with low cloud swirling about the valley. The ponies stood huddled together under a tree, water streaming off their backs in miniature waterfalls. It was no day for crossing Black Sail Pass and there was nothing for it but to stay where I was. A great dollop of hot porridge dispelled some of the gloom, but, by ten o'clock, with no sign of the rain easing, I was becoming really agitated. Earlier visitors to Wasdale had suffered the same frustrations. I once read a poetic plea written in the visitors' book at the Wastwater Hotel by a Miss Knowles, in 1869.

> Oh, Wasdale, where are thy charms
> That poets have found in thy face?
> Better dwell in the midst of alarms
> Than stay in this watery place.

In one of the bags I found a crumpled copy of my local newspaper and, for the first time in ten years, I read every word in it. Branches of the Mothers' Union all over the country were up in arms about the law on abortion. They also objected to young people being given access to contraceptives, arguing that more emphasis should be placed on improving moral standards. How right they are. But how sadly out of touch. I felt sorry for the lady who had a lapse of memory and left a well-known Whitehaven store, forgetting she was wearing three of their coats under her own. From the long list of solemn notices it seemed that the population of Cumberland was being dispatched faster than it was being hatched, and I worked out that if it continued at the same rate, in a few years the true Cumbrian would be as extinct as the one-time famous Cumberland pig. The sports page devoted a lot of space to pigeon racing and it reminded me of a story about the managing director of a company that had moved from a fashionable area in the south of England, to one of the new industrial estates in West Cumberland. Being a bit of a social climber, he was delighted when asked if he would be president of the local flying club. He could see himself zooming over the fells at the controls of a shiny Cessna or Chipmunk, and downing his gin in the club lounge with cries of 'wizard prang!' The evening of his first meeting came and, bursting with excitement, he entered the hall, only to find it full of cages and cooing birds. The flying club he had accepted presidency of was a pigeon flying club.

At midday the rain stopped and I shot out of the tent to see if there was a chance of leaving. The cloud hung heavy over Mosedale and Black Sail, but it had moved higher up the fellside and shafts of sunlight shone through here and there. I decided to go, and lost no time in packing the bags. The fly-sheet was saturated and as heavy as lead, but it had kept the driving rain off the tent and had proved its worth. The ponies were miserable and reluctant to move, but by the time we had passed Wastwater Hotel and started up Mosedale they had warmed up and were full of life. With yesterday's performance still fresh in my mind, I took a long time getting Jewel through a narrow gate onto the open fell. As we splashed our way through swollen becks and picked a way through patches of bog, a weak sun managed to chase the cloud up onto the high tops. Ahead, the long ribbon of the pass, green at first, but rapidly deteriorating into boulders and scree, climbed and twisted its way to a low point on the ridge between Pillar and Kirk Fell. The pack was having an off day and drove me frantic, first slipping to one side, then the other. At a point where the path fords Gatherstone Beck the ground was steep and badly eroded and, leading the ponies up it, I happened to look back down the valley. A virtual wall of water was bearing down on us like an express train. I urged the ponies on, but the pack was heeling and throwing Jewel off balance. She was frightened by the roaring water in the beck and I was busy trying to coax her across when, with a tremendous clap of thunder, the storm was upon us. Jewel reared and fought to get away, as I clung desperately to hold on to her and Thor. The rain lashed into us and the crack of the thunder was ear-splitting. Trying to hold the ponies from bolting, I slipped off a rock and went over my knees in icy water. I was past caring, I was soaked to the skin anyway. With the ponies doing their best to pull me in half, there was no time to mess about with waterproofs. Thor reared and plunged as the thunder echoed about the valley and poor Jewel was so terrified she made a dash across the beck. As she dragged me forward the lead rope caught on the pack and it keeled right over into the water. I could do nothing but cling to the ponies for dear life. They were mad with fright and I felt my arms would be torn from their sockets at any moment. A furious hailstorm followed the rain and a barrage of ice chips beat into my face like a million needles. With a final clap of thunder the storm passed over and an apologetic sun appeared nervously from behind a thick cloud. My hands were so cold I could not untie the knots holding the pack and I had to cut the ropes. Water poured from the bags as I heaved the saddle out of the water and I was very worried about my spare clothes and sleeping-bag. Both were well wrapped in polythene, but the packs had been lying in the beck for at least ten minutes and I felt sure water must have seeped through. I was too cold to start opening bags to check, so I jumped up and down like a madman for a while to get my circulation going. My feet felt a lot warmer when I had squeezed the water out of my socks and, although I was soaked to the skin, providing I kept moving I knew I would be all right, so I rushed around getting the ponies tacked up. They calmed down once the storm passed and, with the sodden pack lashed tight, we pressed on for the summit. The last two or three hundred feet were very loose and slippy and I was busy negotiating a particularly awkward section when Jewel whinnied. I looked back and my heart sank. The damned pack-saddle had fallen off again, and gone completely under her belly. What a position to be in. The angle of the slope was about forty-five degrees, Thor was panicking and trying to take off, and Jewel, who could not move, was having her neck stretched by the strain on the lead rope. To cap it all the rain started sluicing down with renewed vigour. With a short rope attached to Thor's head-collar, I hobbled him by tying it to a foreleg, and there he perched like a big black statue, backside up the slope and head down it, unable to move. I had one hell of a struggle extricating Jewel from the pack-saddle. The girth was bar taut and I could not unfasten the buckles. To add to the problem she was rolling her eyes and trying to jump over the pack. I was worried that if she lost her footing she would fall into the gully below. The weather was worsening, so there was no time to lose. I cut the buckles off the girth strap and the saddle fell away. With Jewel hobbled in a similar fashion to Thor, I made a makeshift girth and heaved everything back onto the saddle as best I could. Ominous black clouds drifted over Kirk Fell and it began to snow heavily. This was a real hazard. If it balled up under the ponies' shoes it would be very dangerous and I drove them on as fast as I could. Such is the crazy British climate that, on reaching the summit of the pass, the clouds cleared, a strong sun broke through and we basked in the warmth. I steamed like a Turkish bath as the heat penetrated my saturated clothing. I was so relieved and happy at having reached the top I hardly noticed that my boots oozed water at every step.

Menacing storm clouds were building up over Red Pike and Pillar as we rested, so I quickly got the ponies together for the descent into Ennerdale. Far below I could see the tiny building of Black Sail Youth Hostel, where I hoped to camp for the night. The path on the Ennerdale side of Black Sail Pass had deteriorated badly with the action of frost and rain, aided by countless thousands of boots. Descending it with one pony is awkward enough, but with two it was absolutely hair-raising and it was not only the ponies who were snorting with fear by the time we clambered down the last rock pitch to the grass by the edge of the forest.

The clouds closed in and the rain beat down again, as we followed the Forestry Commission's fence down to the River Liza. Ennerdale looked bleak and dreary as the rain swept in thick grey waves from the dark face of Great Gable. The whole head of the valley seemed to be an unending expanse of bog, and it was heavy going for the ponies, as they floundered across the acres of spongy moss. A blustery wind funnelled through the fells and drove icy rain through my already saturated clothes, while I fought to pitch the tent on a reasonably level piece of ground. As we were on open fell I got out the thick leather hobbles I had made and strapped them on to the ponies' forelegs. They seemed happy enough hopping from one patch of grass to another, so I flung the kit-bags into the tent and piled in after them. Stripping off my wet clothes, I got into my sleeping-bag and, after a hot meal of tinned chicken and rice, several cups of coffee and a tot of rum, the world looked a lot rosier. The wind increased to gale force and blasted the tent with such ferocity I felt sure that the canvas would be torn to shreds. Sleep was impossible and I lay listening to the wind screeching down from the crags like an army of tormented souls. Towards midnight it dropped and I opened the tent door to find the ground white with snow. It was bitterly cold, but dressed in all my spare clothes, with a wool balaclava pulled down over my face, I generated a lovely heat and drifted into a blissful, undisturbed sleep.

I slept late the following morning and it was nine o'clock before I forced myself out of the warm fug in the sleeping-bag. The snow had disappeared, but thick cloud hung low, draping the valley in a thick, clinging mist, so cold it seemed to penetrate to the bone. It was not a morning for stripping to the waist and splashing in the river, so I made do with rubbing my face with yesterday's wet shirt. I was anxious to check the ponies before I had breakfast, but I was faced with an awful decision. If I wore my dry trousers and got wet again I would have nothing to change into, yet to wear wet trousers would be agony. Deciding I would rather have dry trousers to wear at night, I reached for the wet ones lying in a soggy, crumpled heap at the door of the tent. I squeezed as much water out of them as I could, then gingerly drew them over my legs. The pores of my skin, warm and relaxed from the sleeping-bag, snapped shut like limpets and I shuddered as the frozen material was drawn upwards. Fastening the trousers round my waist, I felt as if I had been lowered into a freezer and I was worried that my future function in life might be reduced to guarding the doors of a harem. Pulling on my sodden boots I crawled out of the tent and did a war-dance to get my blood circulating. I could not see the ponies, so I hunted around the hillocks above the campsite, expecting to find them grazing peacefully. There was no sign of them. I searched the area almost to the foot of Great Gable, but there was not so much as a hoofprint. Greatly puzzled, and becoming a bit worried, I went back to the tent and searched the forestry fence for a gap where they might have got through. There was no gap. I climbed higher towards the foot of Black Sail Pass and, to my delight, came across a hoofprint, but only Jewel's. I could not understand how she had traversed such rough ground, but on a clump of heather I found the answer – a chewed up piece of leather, that had once been a hobble. The erratic line of prints continued upwards, but there was no sign of the ponies. I sniffed my way over rocks and heather like a bloodhound and found Thor's prints coming from another direction. I now had two sets of hoofprints to follow, but my joy was dampened by the way they were heading relentlessly towards the top of the pass. Up and up I toiled, the tent and breakfast fast receding into the distance. When I reached the summit and Mosedale came into view I was reciting a long list of nasty words describing Fell ponies, in particular one large idiot called Thor and his scatter-brained girlfriend, Jewel. I should have suspected they were up to something when I hobbled them the previous night. They stood nose to nose in a huddle and when I went over to them Thor adopted his look of downtrodden innocence, which usually brought little girls with titbits and cries of 'Oh, what a poor old pony'. As soon as I moved away the noses came together.

'I've had enough of this trekking caper, Jewel. What do you say we make a run for it when he's asleep. I was put on this earth to look attractive in a field, not to go clambering over mountains like a damned goat.'

'I'm with you all the way,' replied Jewel. 'All I want to do is have babies and if they'd provided me with something better than that old fool of a worn-out stallion I would be bringing up a nice colt or filly instead of carrying that awful pack-saddle.'

'O.K.,' said Thor, 'we'll quietly graze our way up towards the path and while you've got your head down, chew as hard as you can at the hobble. Once we are free we'll follow our tracks and be in Ravenglass in no time.'

And that is what they did, except, thankfully, a gate stopped them by the Wastwater Hotel.

I was in a foul mood by the time I caught up with them and they listened with ears flat back against their heads while I

cursed and shouted. Despite my rage, I could not help being
full of admiration for the way they had freed themselves and
crossed the rocky pass in the pitch dark and howling gale. As
if to help spread peace, a bright sun broke the cloud and
warmed our backs as we plodded once more over Black Sail.
Gripping his thick mane, I rode Thor bare-back, with Jewel
in tow, on the end of a piece of baler twine, and at two
o'clock that afternoon I sat outside the tent eating a belated
breakfast, while the pair of them stood by the forest fence,
festooned with rope, hardly able to move a muscle.

Thick cloud rolled down off Pillar, bringing a steady drizzle,
as I lashed the kit-bags onto the pack saddle. The River Liza,
swollen with rain, roared and foamed over the ford and I had
a few anxious moments as the ponies went deep into the
water and fought to get a grip on the smooth stones of the
river bed. Safely across, they picked their way along a stony
path by the edge of the forest, towards the tiny youth hostel.
Moisture dripped from the branches of the dark conifers and
the musky scent of spruce hung heavy in the air. We rested
for a few minutes in the lea of the hostel wall, while I adjusted
the pack. Once a shepherd's bothy, the old building has
changed little over the years and is one of the few real youth
hostels left. Originally founded with the purpose of
providing cheap accommodation for impecunious youngsters,
the Youth Hostels Association, like so many organizations,
has lost sight of its ideals and geared itself to the motorist
seeking a cheap holiday. Hostel grounds once filled with
Raleighs and Sunbeams, are now cluttered with Fords and
Minis and, instead of maintaining an overnight charge
common to every hostel, the association has evolved a
system of tariffs according to amenities provided. The YHA
handbook resembles a Michelin Guide, with its star system
of grading, and instead of a map and compass, the modern
hosteller needs a pocket calculator. Lonely outposts, such as

Black Sail, accessible only to walkers, cyclists and horse-riders, remain as memorials to the true spirit of hostelling.

Beyond the hostel, the thin brown ribbon of Scarth Gap Pass climbed high above the forest, disappearing into the cloud between High Crag and Haystack. As we approached the foot of the long climb which would take us to Buttermere, some absent-minded god opened the wrong valve and water cascaded in vicious torrents, sending us scurrying for the shelter of the trees. Hailstones as big as golf balls bent the branches of the trees almost to snapping point and made the ponies stamp and snort as they thumped into their unprotected faces. It would have been asking for trouble to go over the pass in that weather, so we set off down through the forest in front of the storm, like pebbles driven along the river bed. Water spilled from my saturated boots and dribbled from the stirrups in a continuous stream, but, although I was soaked to the skin, I was tolerably warm.

The track through Ennerdale Forest is often described as being long and tedious, but to me it was a joy. Despite the awful weather the going was easy for the ponies and I could relax in the saddle without having to worry about bogs, or to lead the way through boulders and scree. The Forestry Commission has been on the receiving end of a great deal of criticism over the way they virtually took over Ennerdale and carpeted the fellsides with rows of conifers, where sheep once grazed. Whatever the arguments were against establishing the forest in the 1920s, there is no doubt in my mind that what the commission is doing today is good, and in the best interest of those who seek peace and beauty in a valley where the motor car is not welcome.

A mile or two down the forest road the rain eased off, then petered out altogether. The low clouds began to lift and a gap in the trees revealed the full magnificence of Pillar Rock, suspended above the forest like a fairy castle in ancient mythology. A shaft of sunlight pierced the mist and, as the air on the valley floor warmed, it rose, and carried the clouds with it, high above the fells. Unhindered, the afternoon sun beat down with a golden glow and I basked in its warmth as we jogged steadily on between the steaming trees.

At Gillerthwaite, the warden of the youth hostel gave me the name of the farmer who tenanted the land, so I phoned him and got permission to camp in a field at Low Gillerthwaite Farm. The farmhouse had been converted to a field study centre by a college association from Leeds and the warden, Mike Rollison, came over while I was pitching camp and offered me the use of the centre's drying room and toilets. With my wet clothes festooned about Mike's drying-room, and having enjoyed the luxury of a wash and shave in hot water, I cracked open another tin of chicken and rice. Well laced with curry powder, it seared its way into my stomach and soon had the dampness of the past two days running for its life. The ponies, having almost forgotten what real grass looked like, sniffed cautiously then, as the light dawned, tore into it, hardly pausing for breath. I lay back against a stone wall, watching the sun sink behind Pillar. It was utter peace, and in so beautiful a setting it was difficult to imagine that, in 1841, deer inhabiting the old Ennerdale Forest almost brought starvation to the occupants of the two farms at Gillerthwaite. At harvest time the deer came in droves, into the very field where I was sitting, and ate their way through the sheaves of corn stooked for drying. The farmers tried chasing them with dogs, but at night they returned to wreak more havoc. In desperation, old scythe blades and pitchforks were fastened in gaps in the walls, facing inwards, towards the fields. The deer got in all right, but when chased by the dogs they were impaled on the spikes. Not very pleasant, but in the days before social security, no crop meant no food for the dales' farmer and his family.

Weary after the day's escapades, my head hardly reached the saddle-blanket pillow before I was fast asleep.

CHAPTER FOUR
Gillerthwaite to Gatesgarth

A fussy little chaffinch perched on the tent-pole, chirping away for all he was worth, woke me early the next morning. As I opened the tent door he shot off, but looking out I could see the reason for his excitement. It was an absolutely gorgeous morning, without a cloud in the sky. The first rays of the sun lit the fell tops and as it rose a pink glow slid down over the crags to lighten the sombre green of the vast carpet of spruce. A heavy dew had turned the grass to silver and exposed delicate spiders' webs, hung about walls and fences. Above Red Pike a buzzard hovered effortlessly, keeping a watchful eye on a pair of ravens flapping lazily over the field, the 'pronk pronk' of their morning chat echoing up the silent valley. As the sun climbed higher a cuckoo stirred into life and flitted from tree to tree, sounding its familiar call.

The ponies were lying together in a corner of the field, so I went across to see them. Instead of climbing to their feet and moving off as they usually did, they allowed me to sit with them and brush the mud off their coats. To be trusted by an animal is the finest compliment a man can be given and to feel a friendship developing with my ponies was a great joy. Curse and scold if you must, but never hurt a pony or the trust will vanish forever.

It was eleven o'clock before I left Gillerthwaite, but I was in no hurry. The weather looked settled at last, and it was so warm I was able to tie my anorak to the saddle and feel the sun on my arms. Riding along the side of Ennerdale Water was superb, the track winding round little bays and headlands, bordered with silver birch, sparkling in the bright

sunlight. Small clearings among the birch were a mass of
wild flowers and Herdwick sheep nibbled contentedly while
their lambs chased each other in and out of the trees. The air
was crisp and clear and the morning so breathtakingly
beautiful it almost defies description. Anyone familiar with
the Lake District will know what I mean.

The Forestry Commission's car park at Bowness Knott
marked the end of Ennerdale Forest. The surfaced road
beyond was scarcely wide enough for a car, so I put Jewel on
a very short lead rope. Walking behind Thor she would
always keep to his right side, which meant that on a narrow
road she would be in the middle of it. Both ponies were
nervous as several cars approached, so I led them the mile or
so to Whins Farm and the start of the bridleway to Floutern
Tarn and Buttermere. It was a great relief to leave the
soulless tarmac behind and enter a delightful stony lane,
overhung with hawthorn and bramble. In days gone by,
farm carts and pack-ponies would have gone this way, but as
the tractor and motor vehicle took over, the lane was
abandoned to nature and wild hedgerows overflowed with
red campion, bluebells, and delicate herb Robert.

At the end of the lane, a gate led onto open fell and a wide
path of springy turf zigzagged comfortably upwards,
making for an obvious gap between Herdus and Banna Fell.
The ponies were in great form and belted along as if they had
heard on the horsy grapevine that someone was giving away
free oats in Buttermere. At the top of the climb the path
levelled out and below was a marvellous aerial view from
Bowness Point, across Ennerdale Water and the coastal
plain, to the Solway Firth and the rolling hills of Galloway.

Approaching Floutern Tarn, a wire fence barred our way
and although a couple of stout iron posts had once
supported a gate, it had long since disappeared and the gap
blocked with wire netting and barbed wire. I looked at the
map and checked my position. Sure enough, I was on a

bridleway, so out came the pliers and I cut through the wire, folding it back to get the ponies through. With the wire fastened in position again, we continued on past Floutern Tarn, sliding down steep grass by the roaring torrent of Mosedale Beck, to the edge of a seemingly endless bog. The more I looked the less I liked it, so tying the ponies to an old fence post, I waded into a mire of rushes and trembling bog to try and find a way through. With the aid of a long stick I prodded around until I worked out a route which I hoped would see us across this nightmare to the hard ground at the foot of Gale Fell. Turning to collect the ponies my heart sank at the sight of a huge mass of vile black cloud, boiling across the sun. The message was loud and clear, we were in for one hell of a storm. Grabbing Thor's reins I dragged him into the swamp and, with Jewel splashing behind, fought my way towards the cairn of stones I had made to mark the dry ground. Full of apprehension, the ponies tried to turn back, but I bellowed at them to keep going and, in a wild flurry of hooves, we clambered to safety. They wanted to shake but there was no time. The storm was almost upon us and the first drops of rain thudded against Thor's saddle as I drove the ponies at a crazy pace for the Buttermere valley. Hurrying through a small patch of wet ground, Thor crossed without difficulty, but, hearing a gasp, I swung round to find Jewel up to her belly in thick slime. The storm had us trapped. With a terrifying roar a triumphant clap of thunder resounded round the fells and a savage deluge of water tore into us like a waterfall. Jewel struggled to free herself, but only sank deeper into the mud. Flinging Thor's reins round his forelegs to stop him bolting, I crawled into the icy slime to try and release the pack-saddle, but the buckles were too far down. The lashing rain turned the area into a quagmire and as I lay full length, struggling with the girth, freezing water soaked me to the skin. I reached deep into the mud with both hands, but I could not release the buckles. There was only one answer – to cut through the girth. My knife was in a bag on Thor's saddle and I was reaching for it when Jewel suddenly gave a tremendous heave and with a noise like water pouring down a gigantic plug-hole, pulled herself out of the bog, onto hard ground. Brave little Jewel. I gave her a big hug as she stood regaining her strength, chunks of peat slopping on to the ground, washed down by the rain. Miraculously, she was none the worse for the ordeal and chewed nonchalantly on a clump of heather. I was so cold I could hardly tie Jewel's lead rope to my saddle, but my usual blood-warming war-dance would have to wait. The rain had forced the cloud down off the fells and reduced the visibility to less than a hundred yards. Having no proper path to follow, I set a compass course to bring us to a point were the map showed the bridlepath crossing Black Beck, before descending to Crummock. On we trekked, through the rain, sparks flying from the ponies' shoes as we struggled to keep a straight course through patches of boulders and scree. Ahead, I could hear running water and suddenly the mist lifted to reveal the head of Black Beck and the grey expanse of Crummock Water below. Leaving the ponies hobbled, I went forward to find a crossing place. I had hardly gone ten yards when I was over my boots in a bog. It was the same higher upstream and, after desperate tramping about for half an hour, it was obvious there was no way I was going to get the ponies through that glutinous mass. The rain dripped off the map as I searched for an alternative route, but there was none to be found. We were well and truly caught between two fearsome expanses of bog, and I roundly cursed those who allowed ancient bridleways to deteriorate to such a degree. While swearing made me feel better, it was not solving the problem, so I set about reconnoitring the fellside for a way down. Black Beck was out of the question, both sides were steep and rocky, and ended in a series of waterfalls. Following an old fence line as it dropped steeply to Scale Beck, I found a rocky gully which looked promising. Rain was pouring down it in miniature waterfalls, but if the ponies could negotiate one awkward step we would soon be safely in the valley.

When you have been with ponies day in and day out you find yourself talking to them as if they were human beings. They do not always do as you ask them, but their ears swivel round and they certainly listen. I talked to Thor and Jewel all day. Sometimes coaxing or urging them on, perhaps swearing at them when they were being silly, or maybe just sitting with them at the end of a day and making conversation. Somehow by the inflexions of my voice, they understood what I was saying and the response was remarkable.

I gathered up the ponies and led them to the edge of the gully and let them look down it.

'Look, you two,' I said, 'we are in a jam and if you get down there I'll give you a Mars Bar each.'

Thor peered over then backed hastily away.

'Coward,' I growled at him.

Jewel was particularly fond of Mars Bars and, gazing down at the drop, I am quite sure she would have launched herself into space had I not grabbed her lead rope. Removing the pack and saddle, I gingerly led her forward. She slid down on her forelegs as far as a small ledge, then gave a mighty leap and jumped about five feet to the ground. Tying her quickly to the fence I went back for Thor. He kept looking down, but he would not budge.

'Right,' I said, 'if you won't come, then we'll go without you,' and climbing down to Jewel, I started to lead her away. That did the trick. Whether it was the thought of losing his Mars Bar or Jewel, I will never know, but with a shrill whinny he stuck out his feet and tobogganed down the rock face like a great wingless Pegasus.

By the impressive gorge of Scale Force, a rambling club watched spellbound, while the ponies had their reward. Jewel munched her Mars Bar quietly, but Thor, ever an exhibitionist, rolled his round his tongue and stuck it out of the side of his mouth like a Churchillian cigar.

It was now 6 p.m. and, not having eaten since breakfast, my mouth felt like blotting-paper. The rain eased a little, but more black cloud, scudding across the sky from the southwest, warned of evil things to come. I had intended to camp by Buttermere village, but the whole place swarmed with tents and caravans, so I pressed on for Gatesgarth Farm, at the Honister end of Buttermere. The National Trust had chained and locked the gate leading into Burtness Wood, so I lifted it off its hinges and dragged it to one side. It is amazing how many rights of way are impassable on National Trust property and, though charged with preserving our national heritage, they tend to overlook the fact that an ancient right of way is just as much a part of that heritage as any listed building, however lacking in prestige value.

The black clouds disgorged their load and the rain pelted down, helped along by a fierce wind. I was thankful to be in the shelter of the trees, as the gale whined overhead, and, although the rain poured off the branches, my clothes had reached saturation point long ago, another few gallons was not going to make any difference. The ponies were worn out as we approached Gatesgarth and the pace became slower and slower. At the farm, Tom Richardson was kindness itself, and with Thor and Jewel chewing away at fresh grass, I pitched camp in the shelter of a wall. Mrs Richardson took all my wet clothes into the house to dry, and, snug inside the tent, a feast of corned beef and rice was soon bubbling away on the primus stove. Wrapped in my sleeping-bag, drowsy with the effects of a large noggin of rum, I hardly heard the gale-lashed rain drumming on the canvas.

* * *

When I woke the next morning the gale had blown itself out, but it was still pouring with rain. Quite by chance I had pitched the tent on a mound of grass and, looking out, I found I was surrounded by a wide moat. The whole field was waterlogged and a long line of ewes with bedraggled lambs, huddled against the wall for shelter. Out of about twenty tents in the field, half had blown down and the occupants, having spent a miserable night cramped in their cars, were emerging, bleary-eyed and stiff, to gather up the debris. A company of soldiers were camped quite close to me and, observing that four small tents had been pitched at a discreet distance from the main body, I was amused to discover I was sharing the officers' mess. I laughed to myself as my memory jumped back twenty odd years to when, resplendent in best uniform, I presented myself before a collection of tired-looking individuals at an officer selection board.

'I'm afraid you are just not officer material,' frowned a beetroot-faced wing commander, who, only a few weeks before, had sentenced me to seven days' detention for leading a successful raid on a nearby Army camp and stealing the regimental cannon. Actually, the Army were very sporting and when we returned the hallowed museum piece, gave us a slap-up dinner in the NAAFI. Beetroot face was not amused and, having intoned the standard charge of 'action prejudicial to conduct and good order of the Royal Air Force', slapped me in the cooler for a week.

I watched the sergeant major strut about rousing the men out of the tents, streams of water running down their faces as they lined up for inspection. Moustache bristling, he briefed the squad on the day's route, then, with a final gem of wisdom, as if he had discovered it all by himself, he announced, 'Today it is raining and you will get wet.'

Senior NCOs do not seem to have changed much in twenty years.

Around 1 p.m. the rain eased off and I climbed out of the

tent to stretch my legs and have a look at the ponies. They came to the gate when I called so I took the opportunity to check them for saddle galls and loose shoes. Everything was fine, and, leaving them a biscuit apiece, I set off to look at the old pack-horse route running along Warnscale Bottom. In the early days of the great quarry on Honister Crag, slate was carried down on the backs of ponies and a path was cut into the hillside and surfaced with blocks of stone. The path from Gatesgarth was level and firm, at first, but at a collection of ruins, once the stables for the pack-ponies, it climbed steeply upwards to a series of magnificent waterfalls, high up in Warnscale Beck. Swinging away from the beck at a rocky platform with a sheer drop to the valley below, the path continued up towards Dubs Quarry, but I was terribly disappointed to discover that a landslip had carried a section of it away. On a nice dry day, with one pony, it would have presented no difficulty, but with water pouring from every crack and the rocks as slippy as a grease pan, to try and handle two ponies in such an airy situation, would have risked their lives unnecessarily. Tomorrow, I would have to take the road over Honister Pass.

A watery sun was struggling through the clouds, turning the pools of water to gold, as I returned to the campsite. In the farmyard, Joss Richardson, Tom's brother, was working with some sheep, so I stopped for a chat.

'Awful weather, Joss.'

'Aye,' he replied, 'it's been one of the worst lambings we've had in years, and if this weather doesn't improve it'll be the worst this century.'

'What you could do with,' I said, 'is some sort of gadget that will forecast the weather months in advance.'

He laughed at the idea and then, rubbing his chin in thought, said, 'Well you know, there was a bit of a tale used to be told, about an old dales' farmer who always worried about the weather. One of his neighbours said if he got himself a barometer and hung it in the kitchen, he would be able to tell the weather in advance and get his hay in safely. Well, the old chap got a barometer, but, although it was pouring with rain, the barometer needle said "fine". Each day he went to it, but it was always the same. The barometer said "fine", but outside it poured with rain. In a rage, the farmer tore it from the wall and stalked out into the yard. Holding it high above his head, he shouted, "Look there, you bloody fool, now will you believe your own eyes!" '

The soldiers departed noisily for the local pub as I was preparing my evening meal, so, after I had eaten and cleaned up, I crawled into my sleeping-bag, hoping to be asleep before they returned. A last look at the sky promised a nice day, but the weather god had broken his promise so often I had given up believing the signs.

CHAPTER 5

Unfriendly Watendlath

I was up early the next morning and, by eight o'clock, I had the bags packed and ready to go. A thick layer of clouds covered the fells, but it was warm and muggy and looked like being a nice day. It was a Sunday and I wanted to be well on my way before the sun brought out the motorists. The best of intentions often go astray and, having called at the farm to thank the Richardsons for their kindness, it was gone eleven o'clock before I finally emerged from the kitchen, full of tea and cake. By now the road was fairly busy and I had to keep Jewel on a short rope to stop her wandering into the middle of the road. Fortunately, the morning crop of motorists were friendly and considerate, passing us carefully, with lots of cheery waving. The sun broke through, quickly dispersing the cloud and in the unaccustomed heat the ponies plodded up the smooth tarmacadam sweating with exertion. On the summit of the pass we rested and, while the ponies snatched at the short grass, I took some photographs of Honister Crag. Towering almost 2,000 feet above Buttermere, it is an awe-inspiring sight. In the days of the Border raiders it was often the scene of fierce fighting.

In one raid, the Graemes, a noted border clan, stole all the sheep and cattle in Borrowdale and made their escape over Honister Pass. They were hotly pursued by the dalesmen and a bloody battle took place, in which the clan chief's son was killed. The old chief was stricken with grief at the loss and the boy's body was buried high on Honister Crag, in a grave marked with his bonnet, claymore and shield.

It was now well past noon and the trickle of cars had increased to a torrent as we began the descent into

Borrowdale. I had planned to join a bridleway just below
Honister Youth Hostel, which would take me to Grange, but
Tom Richardson said that two riders who had stayed with
him recently had been unable to get through because a bank
had fallen away. Another piece of neglected heritage, in
danger of becoming just a memory. I was irritated at having
to keep to the road and the antics of the idiotic motorists did
not make me feel any better. The leading car in a long line
crawling up from Seatoller suddenly stopped on a blind bend
and the driver and his wife got out to take photographs,
completely oblivious to the chaos they were causing. The
enraged drivers of the other cars sounded their horns with
annoyance and the cacophony of noise echoed around the
crags like trumpets outside the walls of Jericho. Even the
ponies interrupted their chewing to stare at this human
madness. Eventually, the second car in the line managed to
squeeze past and the others followed, with revving engines,
screeching tyres and a series of kangaroo leaps. The crazy
convoy tore down into Buttermere and peace returned. A
skylark soared above with his chirpy little song and the
happy cries of children playing, drifted up from a beck below
the road.

It was gorgeously warm and a treat to ride with shirt
sleeves rolled up, my body soaking up heat instead of water.
A blue haze hung over the wooded valley as we skated down
the last bit of near vertical asphalt into the tiny hamlet of
Seatoller, and in the car park the ponies attacked a hedgerow
of long, sweet grass.

Because of its high annual rainfall, Borrowdale has been
called the Devil's Chamber Pot, but, for a change, Old Nick
was suffering from dehydration. Once noted for its gloomy
winters, due to the high crags shutting out the sun, legend
has it that the inhabitants tried to build a wall across the dale
to imprison the cuckoo, so that they would always have good
weather. When the cuckoo flew over the wall and escaped

one of the builders shouted, 'By God, Willy, another course of stones and we would have held it. We mun work faster next year.'

The car park swarmed with people, so Thor put on his best down-trodden look and in no time the pair of them were surrounded by old ladies and children, offering crisps and sweets. I could not bear to witness such blatant scrounging, so I escaped into a nearby café for a mug of coffee and a sandwich. Some time ago, BBC North East did a programme about tourism in the Lake District and in it Jake Kelly said that to buy a cheese sandwich in Grasmere you needed a banker's credit card. To eat in Seatoller, you need to own the bank. Two cheese sandwiches and a cup of coffee cost me over a pound.

The ponies were unhappy about losing the attention of a coachload of adoring old ladies and dragged their feet as we left the car park. A dear old soul thrust a large bag of peppermint humbugs into my hands, 'For the sweet little ponies,' she said, 'in case they get hungry on the journey.'

Sweet little ponies, my foot! In half an hour they had gorged themselves so full of crisps, biscuits, sweets and cakes I could hardly fasten the girths.

The mile or so of road between Seatoller and Rosthwaite was jammed with cars and coaches and I breathed a huge sigh of relief when we clattered over the stone bridge crossing Stonethwaite Beck at the foot of the long climb to Watendlath. The sun was high in the sky and even in the shelter of the trees, the heat was so intense the ponies were lathered in sweat as they slipped and staggered up the deeply eroded path. At Birkett's Leap the ground levelled out and, under the welcome shade of a large oak, I halted and rested the ponies. They did not bother to graze, but stood with drooping eyelids, tails swishing occasionally to flick away a persistent fly. After the freezing rain and wind of the past week, it was sheer bliss to lie against the rough bark of the tree, basking in the warmth. The woodland aroma of dry soil, moss and bracken drifted deliciously into my nostrils, as I lay close to the ground, and a wave of relaxation swept over me, releasing the springs of my overwound mind. I was looking forward to camping at Watendlath. A tiny community perched on glacial debris above the Borrowdale valley, it was once an important converging point for the many pack-horse routes, radiating in all directions. It once boasted an inn, where the pack-horse drivers could enjoy an evening of merriment, safe from footpads and other rogues who haunted the fells, eager to relieve them of their goods and cash. The inn and the pack-horse trains have long since gone and the economy of the hamlet is largely dependent on the Herdwick sheep.

On the move again, we joined a long crocodile of walkers toiling up the rounded slopes of the aptly named Puddingstone Bank. The heat was too much for some and they dropped out to sprawl on the grass, mopping beads of sweat from steaming brows and slurping great gulps from bottles of fizzy lemonade. As we overtook the leaders, they waved cheerily and quipped, 'Any chance of a lift, mate?' or 'Can we hang onto the ponies' tails?' But they were soon well behind and we had the fell to ourselves. At the top of the climb, an easy path crossed a flat plateau and, despite the haze, there was a fantastic view across Watendlath valley to Armboth Fell, and south to Langstrath and the Langdale Pikes. Watendlath Tarn, shimmering in the sun, beckoned like an oasis as, hot and thirsty, we began the descent to the valley. Centuries of rain had gouged deep ruts into the path, and while busy guiding Thor over a particularly rough section, Jewel set off along another path which took her fancy. What she did not know was that the path she was following went up and Thor and I were going down. It was only when the lead rope went taut above my head that I discovered I was holding onto a four-legged, hairy kite. I had to coax the little pest down a steep bank and she looked so upset when I swore at her, I gave her one of the old lady's humbugs, which she crunched happily as we continued on our way.

From a distance the collection of cottages, huddled together for protection, gives the impression of a forgotten hamlet, abandoned by time to continue life at its own sleepy pace, but, as the ponies splashed through the ford, it was painfully obvious that, far from being abandoned, Watendlath was very much a part of twentieth-century commercialism. Visitors swarmed everywhere and practically every cottage sold teas, soft drinks and ice-cream. The whole hamlet was one enormous café.

The ponies, having travelled quite a distance in the heat, were showing signs of fatigue, so, leaving them tied to a tree, I called at a farmhouse to ask if I could camp and graze the ponies.

'No, we don't take campers,' said the bearded farmer.

'But it's only for one night,' I urged, 'and the ponies are just about done.'

'Can't help that,' he replied, 'we stopped taking campers last year, they leave too much mess.' He went on, 'In any case, the National Trust own this property and they don't allow camping.'

'Damn the National Trust,' I hissed under my breath, 'they've never been stuck up a fell with tired ponies.' Trying to sound as helpful as I could, I said, 'Look, would you graze the ponies for the night and I'll go up the fell and find a wall to sleep under.'

'Sorry,' was the reply, 'I haven't enough grazing.'

Through the window of the farmhouse I could see the ponies dozing under the tree, little Jewel just longing to get the pack off her back and have a good roll. On the window-sill of the house was a 'Bed and Breakfast' sign, so, in desperation, trying not to think of the dent it would make in my money, I asked if I stayed the night at the farm, would he graze the ponies.

'I'll see if we have a room,' he said sourly, and disappeared into the kitchen. There was a murmur of voices, then he returned, 'Sorry, no vacancies. Best thing you can do is go over the fell to Thirlmere and make for Bridge End Farm. They take campers.'

'What's the ground like on the fell?' I asked.

'Oh, maybe a bit damp, but you'll make it.'

I went out to the ponies and adjusted the pack for the steep climb up Armboth Fell. They gave me a very odd look, but there is no way you can explain to a tired pony the peculiarities of the human race. While I was tightening the girths a car drew up by the farm and a couple got out.

'Let's see if we can get bed and breakfast here,' said the woman, and into the house they went. Emerging a few minutes later, one said to the other, 'It looks a very comfortable room, perhaps we can stay two nights. Let's go for a walk before dinner.'

Muttering unprintable words, I led the ponies up the fellside.

Poor Jewel was really tired and it took a long time to climb the steep, broken path out of the valley. Near the top the pack started to slip and more time was wasted, removing the bags and reloading. Unfriendly Watendlath faded out of sight as the two ponies stumbled over the final rise and plodded wearily across the moorland, towards the heathery summit of High Tore. At first, the path was fairly hard, but after a little way it ended abruptly, leaving us to find a way through a maze of peat hags. We made so many detours, I was beginning to get worried about the time, it had gone seven o'clock and darkness was not far away. At High Tore, long shadows were spreading across the surrounding fells as the sun dipped towards the horizon and the still surface of

Thirlmere was already black as light faded from the valley. Standing head and shoulders above Dollywaggon Pike and the Raise, the rambling mass of Helvellyn burnt with blood-red fire as it caught the last rays of the dying sun. It was a beautiful evening, but looking towards the way we had to go, I felt sick with worry. A huge bog stretched almost to the trees above Thirlmere, and large areas of bright green sphagnum moss glistened ominously amongst the rushes. It was too late to turn back. Armboth and the road were close and we had to make it before dark. Apart from having to make numerous diversions to avoid some nasty looking patches, the going was not as bad as it had first appeared, but both the ponies and I were so tired we became careless. Crossing a patch of what looked like firm heather, Jewel put both forelegs in a hole and sank up to her chest. She struggled to get out and having done so, promptly sank into the same hole with her hind legs. It took half an hour to free her and then only by tying a long rope round Thor's chest and yanking her out by the nose. Pack-saddle adjusted, we set off again, all three of us wet and thoroughly plastered with mud. Hardly had we gone two hundred yards when Thor sank up to his belly. He lay there, too tired to move, and I sat on a clump of heather, too exhausted to help him. Having rested, he gave a couple of mighty heaves and miraculously clambered to safety. The nightmare patch behind us, we descended on firm ground to a gate in a wall. Our problems were not over yet. The gate was too narrow for Jewel to go through, carrying the pack, and the whole load had to be taken off, Jewel led through, and the pack replaced before we could continue. We had been over some rough surfaces since we left Ravenglass, but the path down through that steep wood was so desperate, by the time the last fallen tree has been hauled to one side by Thor, and the last patch of jagged rock agonizingly negotiated, we were shattered.

While we were resting by the side of the road at Armboth, a Landrover pulled up.

'You all right?' said a voice.

'Fine thanks,' I replied. 'We're just resting.'

'Yon ponies look buggered. How far have you come?'

I told him the story.

'Bloody hell!' he exclaimed. 'That's typical, that is. They have a different kind of farming at Watendlath these days. They milk bloody tourists instead of cows!'

Climbing out of the Landrover, he opened the back door and, carrying a bag of dairy nuts across to the ponies, emptied a great heap in front of them.

'There y'are, git that lot down yer.'

Thor and Jewel did not need to be asked twice. Turning to me, the man asked where I was heading and I said Bridge End Farm.

'It's a caravan site really,' said my friend, 'but they might let you in.'

Climbing into the Landrover, he drove slowly away.

'Look after them ponies, now,' he shouted out of the window, 'a couple of good Fells you've got there.'

The ring of the ponies' shoes echoed from the steep crags as we trudged slowly along the road by the side of Thirlmere. The two miles or so to the farm seemed endless, but eventually we rode into the yard and I rang the doorbell. An attractive girl opened the door, looked me up and down, then went for her mother. The farmer's wife looked very dubious when I asked could I camp and graze the ponies for the night, and said she would ask her husband when he returned from checking the sheep. Feeling worn out and miserable, I sat on the kit-bags at the side of the road. It was almost dark and if he would not let me camp I would be in a right fix. I was working out how I could pitch the tent on a grass verge and tie the poines to a hedge, when the farmer appeared in a field close by. He seemed friendly enough and said to turn the ponies loose in the caravan site. Hardly were we through the gate, when Thor backed up to a smart touring van and rubbed his tail against it with such vigour that the van rocked like a boat. A pair of startled faces appeared at the window and I had to rush over and drag the fool away before he got us thrown out into the road. While I was pitching the tent, a lady from a nearby caravan came over with a large mug of tea and some biscuits. She said I looked tired and thought I might like a drink. Never was there a better judge of a situation. I returned the mug later and sat chatting to them in their comfortable caravan. They were a Mr and Mrs Beer, from Coventry, and I shall long remember their kindness.

I was too tired to eat, so I walked down the road to a phone box and rang home to learn that BBC television wanted to film a progress report and would I phone the producer. It was arranged that Bob Armstrong, a cameraman, would meet me at Stanah the following morning, to film us going up Sticks Pass. I could barely keep my eyes open by the time I crawled into my sleeping-bag, and I was soon fast asleep.

The fact that Thirlmere is Manchester's water supply must have stuck in my subconscious, because I had a most peculiar dream about Thor being caught peeing into Thirlmere and he and Jewel ended up in court. The ponies were put in separate boxes, but Thor kicked his to matchwood and pushed in to stand next to Jewel. When questioned, Jewel refused to answer, and chewed through the Bible when it was held up for her to give oath. The judge became very angry with Thor for showing his teeth and jailed him for contempt of court. Having passed sentence, the judge, a large man with a beard, came over to the box and sneered, 'There you silly horse, I'll wipe the smile off your face. What do you think of that then?'

Quick as a flash, Thor whipped round and, lifting his tail,

buried the judge under an enormous heap of droppings. As everyone rushed screaming from the court, I woke up.

CHAPTER 6

Over Sticks Pass to Patterdale

My watch said six o'clock. Outside, a strong wind moaned through the trees and tore at the tent canvas. It did not sound the best of days for going over Sticks Pass to Ullswater, but at least it was not raining. Cranking the primus stove into life, I made a brew of coffee and lay back in the warmth of my sleeping-bag, sipping it slowly. I ached all over from heaving ponies out of bogs, and wished I could lie in, instead of meeting the BBC cameraman. A packet of dried scrambled egg provided breakfast and it tasted a lot better than it looked. I had not seen dried egg powder for years and it was a vast improvement on the dreadful Ministry of Food concoction we were fed at school during the austere days of rationing. A week of eating that and you were never sure whether you needed a laxative or a landmine.

The campsite washroom was empty, so I stripped off and wallowed in the luxury of a hot shower, until all my aches had disappeared down the drain, together with a lot of embarrassingly dirty water. Sheltered from the wind behind a large caravan, I groomed the ponies, raking out a fine compost of dark soil, moss and peat. Thor had a loose shoe, so I hammered the nails home and clenched them tight. The ponies looked remarkably fit. Jewel had lost most of her rough winter coat and developed a healthy-looking sheen. Gone were the tantrums and cussedness and she had proved herself a brave and tough little pony. Thor had shed a lot of surplus fat and was immensely powerful. His only fault was a tendency to panic at times and try to take off, but I had learnt to anticipate this. I had grown very fond of both of them and a bond of friendship had developed between us, through mutual trust and understanding. It was the most rewarding experience of my life.

Waving good-bye to Mr and Mrs Beer, we left the campsite at nine-thirty, with half an hour to spare before we were due to meet Bob Armstrong. The sky was streaked with 'mare's tails', but the wind had dropped to a light breeze and the morning was fresh and clear. Crossing the busy Keswick to Ambleside road was a bit nerve-racking, as streams of cars, lorries and coaches thundered by in terrible haste. In the end we had to make a dash for it, as a coachload of tourists whizzed by, noses pressed to the windows at the sight of a strange figure shooting across the road, towing two protesting ponies.

A narrow road led to the head of the mystical valley of St John's in the Vale and, by the dark bastions of the fairy fortress of Castle Rock of Triermain, the roar of twentieth-century traffic faded as I drifted into the fantasy world of Sir Walter Scott's long poem, 'The Bridal of Triermain'. In the rock lived a fairy called Gwendolen, whose charms caused King Arthur, of Round Table fame, to lose interest in jousting and turn his attention to other pleasures. The great champion of good over evil obviously suffered from the same weaknesses as us lesser mortals and temporarily abandoned the cause to live for three months with Gwendolen in her tower.

> Arthur, of Christendom, the flower,
> Lies loitering in a lady's bower
> The horn, that foemen wont to fear,
> Sounds but to wake the Cumbrian deer.
> Heroic plans in pleasure drowned,
> He thinks not of the Table Round.

The result of this romance was a beautiful daughter called Gyneth who in later years caused the knights to sweat in their armour whenever she appeared and finally put the cat amongst the pigeons by demanding from the King his most illustrious knight as her husband. A trial by jousting was held at Eamont Bridge near Penrith and chivalry was abandoned in the fierce competition to win the princess.

> The spears drew blood, the swords struck flame,
> And horse and man, to ground there came,
> Knights who shall rise no more.
> Gone was the pride the war that graced,
> Gay shields were cleft and crests defaced
> And steel coats riven, and helms unbraced,
> And pennons streamed with gore.

Arthur, horrified by the sight of his brave knights killing each other in a senseless display of manhood, pleaded with his daughter to end the conflict, but, eyes ablaze with the excitement of being the prize of the victor, she refused. The wizard, Merlin, angered by her selfishness, cast her into an enchanted sleep in Castle Rock to 'sleep until a knight shall wake thee'. Gyneth lay imprisoned until Sir Richard de Vaux fought his way through the magic spells cast around the fortress and rescued her, as the blazing walls crumbled around them.

> Gently, lo! the Warrior kneels,
> Soft that lovely hand he steals,
> Soft to kiss and soft to clasp
> But the warder leaves her grasp
> Lightning flashes, rolls the thunder!
> Gyneth startles from her sleep,
> Totters tower and trembles keep,
> Burst the castle walls asunder.

At Stanah there was no sign of Bob Armstrong, but as we

passed a row of cottages a chap leaned over his gate and shouted excitedly, 'Eh, lad, there's a feller from the BBC been looking for you.' As we were talking, Bob arrived and, introductions over, began setting up his camera. The man in the garden had passed the word to his neighbours and quite an audience watched while the camera whirred as I rode bravely for the summit. Unfortunately, they were still there when I rode sheepishly back again, having discovered I was on the wrong path. One of the cottagers put us right and, with Bob sweating under the weight of the camera, we clambered up through a farmyard to the foot of the pass.

Finishing his filming, Bob departed to his car and I adjusted Jewel's breast strap to stop the pack slipping backwards on the incredibly steep slope. The pass climbed a long rib up the side of Stanah Gill and the ponies had a difficult time keeping their feet on the loose surface. The original path had long since been washed away and only an erratic line beaten by the feet of countless walkers, marked the way to the top. The gruelling angle mercifully eased off and in an airy position, looking down sheer into Stanah Gill, we rested. Way below my feet the narrow ribbon of Thirlmere shimmered tantalizingly in the bright sunlight and I was so dry I could have drunk the lot. Lines of impatient toy vehicles competed with each other along the white scar of the new road, as it bludgeoned its way through ancient rock and over green pasture, carrying the eager hordes to the souvenir shops of Keswick and Ambleside. Looking down the steep fellside, it was difficult to imagine how strings of pack-ponies, laden with ore from the mine at Glenridding, could have managed it. In the old days, it was the only way ore could be taken to Keswick for smelting, and, on a wet day, with the surface of the path treacherous with mud, the drivers would have had many an anxious moment before the ponies reached the valley.

As we climbed higher, a raging wind suddenly whistled

down off Helvellyn, flinging us about like tufts of bog cotton. The pack developed a horrible list as Jewel struggled to keep her feet, so I spurred Thor on, towards a walled sheep-pen, for shelter. Close by the wall Thor shied so violently he almost had me off. Cursing, I pulled him round and in the sheep-pen I could see a blue object bobbing up and down. Pressing closer to the wall, I looked over and, to my astonishment, it turned out to be a chap wearing a blue anorak, and nothing else, making passionate love to a girl on the ground. Not wanting to be branded a 'peeping Tom', I was trying to move quietly away when Jewel chose the wrong moment to let out a shrill whinny. The poor chap got such a fright, he overshot his mark, bashing his head on the wall with a terrible thud. A howl of pain followed us as I drove Thor, hell for leather, up the fellside, but it was not the time for practising first aid. If I lingered I might be needing it. The pack hung at a frightening angle as Jewel was dragged into a trot, but I dared not stop. On we flew, leaping ditches and bog, until, with a final lurch, the pack slid off and Jewel nose dived into the heather. Releasing the girth, I heaved the pack free and sat on it, while the two of them wheezed like worn-out bellows.

'Serves you right, you flaming idiot,' I shouted across to Jewel, 'if you'd kept your big mouth shut it wouldn't have happened.'

As she looked at me, showing two rows of shiny teeth, she may have been sucking in air, but I could have sworn she was laughing.

Reaching the summit of the pass, between the Raise and Stybarrow Dod, the wind reached gale force as the venturi effect of the peaks speeded it up. It was not the best place to admire the view, but I paused long enough to watch, as two tiny figures emerged from the sheep-pen, one supporting the other, as they made their way slowly down towards Stanah.

* * *

The rocky gorge of Sticks Gill, on the Ullswater side, was a sharp contrast to the grassy slopes rising above Thirlmere, and we descended the narrow, shale-covered path very slowly. Cut off from the wind, the steep sides of the fells trapped the sun and, having only minutes before been frozen to the marrow, I was now peeling off down to my shirt. At the foot of the gorge, Sticks Gill runs along the floor of a hanging valley, winding through the derelict mine-workings, before plunging vertically into Glenridding. The old pack-horse path follows a similar course, but leaves the beck, to make a less dramatic, but still very steep, descent, zigzagging down the boulder-strewn slopes of Stang End to the old buildings of Greenside Mine.

The pack needed adjusting, so I tied the ponies to a telegraph pole while I balanced the kit-bags. There was no point in letting them graze, no grass could survive among the great heaps of rubble spread everywhere. There was not a soul to be seen and an eerie silence hung over the abandoned sheds of what was once the finest lead mine in the country. Believed to have started in the middle of the seventeenth century, it operated almost continuously, reaching a depth of 3,000 feet below the surface, until it was completely worked out and abandoned in 1962. The office and stores are now used as mountaineering huts and the miners' bothy is a youth hostel. Were a new vein of ore to be found and the mine opened up again, conservationists would be in an uproar, yet for all its dusty image, mining and its generations of mining families, reach back many centuries into history, and are as much a part of Lakeland as the pretty farmhouses we fondly preserve.

A narrow road dropped down past solemn rows of miners' cottages to the gaudy shop fronts and tourist paraphernalia of Glenridding village. People swarmed everywhere and a carpet of ice-cream wrappers, plastic cups and toffee papers blew about like confetti in the draught of passing cars. My first reaction was to get out of the place with all speed, but my food was running low and I needed to stock up. Finding a quiet spot behind the tourist information caravan, I tied the ponies to a fence and, joining the throng of sweating holidaymakers, I fought my way into a crowded shop. By the time I returned, the ponies had attracted a group of little girls, holding out ice-cream cones and offering them licks. I had a feeling something would happen and, sure enough, as one golden-haired beauty of about five years reached up to pat Thor on the nose, the evil Jewel leaned over and snatched the ice-cream out of her hands, downing it in one gulp. There was dead silence for a few seconds, as Goldilocks stared at her empty hand, then slowly great globules of tears trickled down her face.

'The horsy's eaten me ice-cream,' she sobbed, 'the horsy's eaten me ice-cream.'

Her little friends gathered round in sympathy and, one by one, burst into tears, wailing, 'The horsy's eaten Janice's ice-cream.'

They kicked up a terrible racket and passers-by began to give me such odd looks I dashed across to a shop and, having handed out seven chocolate ice-creams at fifteen pence each, peace was restored.

'Jewel,' I said severely, as we rode away from Glenridding, 'you are a greedy pig and if you get stomach-ache it's your own stupid fault.' The only reply was a loud burp.

The coaches carrying the first visitors to this beautiful part of Lakeland were pulled along at a leisurely pace by four smart horses, polished harness flashing in the sunlight, as the iron-shod wheels rumbled over the gravelled road, beneath graceful trees. The passengers had time to appreciate the view and listen to the sounds of the countryside around them. Progress has condensed the power of the horse into a noisy contraption, belching evil-smelling smoke into the clean air, as it pulls the modern coach at frightening speeds along Mr MacAdams' patent surface. Bemused passengers sit behind rows of glass, well protected from fresh air and fragrant trees and grass, heads whipping from side to side like a Wimbledon tennis final as the countryside flashes past. In a week flat they have 'done' the Lake District and return home, trying desperately to remember what they have seen.

By the time we reached Patterdale, I had seen enough motorized coaches to put me off them forever, and was convinced that the drivers were either not used to Lakeland roads or were just plain lunatics. Waiting for an opportunity to overtake, they drove up behind Jewel with revving engines, then with a loud blast on the horn, thundered by, so close on one occasion, the offside bag scratched the side of one chrome-plated monster. In Patterdale village a sign pointed down a lane to Side Farm pony-trekking centre, so, glad for a chance to escape from the noise and fumes, I left the road to the coaches. I was not sure what sort of reception I would get, but felt that a farmer who kept ponies would find a corner for us somewhere. Spying new faces, a bunch of ponies tore across the field to meet us and crowded round, nipping Jewel and trying to kick Thor. I had a worrying minute or two as Thor reared and plunged, but Jewel saved the day by planting a neat pair of hooves under the chin of a big, grey ruffian, who fancied his chances. With a squeal of pain he wheeled away and, tail and mane streaming in the wind, fled to the far side of the field, taking his pals with him. The tenant of the farm, Mike Taylforth and his wife, were really helpful and soon Thor and Jewel were enjoying a roll in soft green grass, while I pitched the tent in a delightful spot overlooking Ullswater. It was an idyllic setting and I lay in my sleeping-bag with the tent door open and watched as darkness settled over the still water and my two faithful friends faded into the night.

The gentle patter of rain on the tent woke me at 7 a.m. and I looked out to find a thick grey mist hanging motionless over the lake. As I made breakfast I was startled to hear one of the ponies coughing and, going out to check, found it was Thor. He seemed lively enough, so I hoped it was nothing more than a slight cold caused by the extremes of weather we had experienced since leaving Ravenglass. Both ponies had endured a good deal of hardship, so I decided to give them a rest for a couple of days while I explored the area. Some months previously, I had written a book about Ravenglass and Peter Caldwell, the brave chap who had illustrated it and put up the money to have it published, was due in Ambleside that day, delivering copies to local bookshops. Instead of languishing in the tent I would go and meet him. Mike Taylforth had a bus time-table and I set off for the village with twenty minutes to spare. At the bus stop the rain bounced off the tarmac, as I huddled under the hood of my anorak, vainly trying to shelter in the lea of a telephone pole. An old gentleman approached, leading a little dog, and we passed the time of day and commented on the weather.

'You know,' he said, 'I do admire you chaps who climb the fells, but the high tops will be dangerous today. Keep low, old chap, keep low,' he advised as he disappeared into the rain. I had not the heart to tell him I was waiting for a bus.

The 'Mountain Goat' bus appeared round a corner and I was delighted to find it was an old Bedford Duple coach, of late 1940s vintage. Hauling back the sliding door I climbed the steps and went back to my boyhood, when every market day I travelled in an identical vehicle that bulged with buxom country ladies, crates of hens, a few geese and large paperbags, overflowing with cauliflowers, enormous juicy plums and sweet-smelling apples. The heavily laden bus groaned its way between farms and cottages, where people got out to a chorus of 'good-bye' and 'see you next week', from the rest of the passengers. Years later, when I lived in the west of Scotland, the same model of bus served the remote community on a once-a-week journey to Inverness. It was by no means uncommon for the driver to load a few sheep in the back and later on, stop by a croft and herd them into a field. In winter, the interior of the bus was warmed by a paraffin heater tied to the front seat. The long journey from Inverness through Glen Moriston to Kintail passed all too quickly, with much laughter and singing. All this has gone now. Bureaucrats, with their regulations and economists, with their facts and figures, have killed the country bus. The efficient, low cost, owner-driven rattle traps were replaced by sleek, expensive mammoths owned by large transport concerns, who soon bleated that they could not make a profit on the country routes and solved the problem by withdrawing the service. The Mountain Goat Bus Company deserves every support in their attempt to bring new lifelines to the Lake District dales.

The old Bedford growled slowly up Kirkstone Pass then flew down the Troutbeck valley and along the shore of Lake Windermere, to Ambleside. Leaving a message at Fred Holdsworth's bookshop for Peter, I found a quiet corner in the library and browsed through a fine collection of books on local history. In an old book about Ambleside I came across a grand tale about a bishop who came to live in the area, many years ago, and purchased several properties, one of which was a public house in Ambleside, called the Black Cock. The landlord, wanting to please his new owner, suggested the bishop's portrait should replace the existing pub sign and the new sign, showing the bishop in hat and wig, was hung over the door to the disgust of the regulars. The landlord of a nearby pub hung the discarded Black Cock sign over the door to tempt the disgruntled customers over to him. The bishop's tenant, frightened of losing custom through the loss of the original sign, hung a board under the bishop's portrait with the inscription 'This is the Old Cock'.

Amongst Thomas de Quincey's flowery prose in

Recollections of the Lakes and Lake Poets, I came across a touching little story about the tragedy of George and Sarah Green, who worked a small farm in Easedale near Grasmere. One cold blustery day in March, they walked over to Langdale to attend a farm sale and while they were there the weather deteriorated and it began to snow heavily. Everyone made for home and although George's friends advised him to keep to the road he was anxious about his six children, left in the care of his nine-year-old daughter, Agnes. With his wife close behind him, he was last seen striking up the fell in the teeth of the gale.

In Easedale the six small children sat round the peat fire listening intently for the return of their parents, but darkness came and there was still no sign of them. Worn out with waiting, they finally toppled into their beds and dropped off to sleep.

During the night the blizzard increased and by morning the children were completely snowed in and unable to go for help. Agnes examined their meagre stock of food and rationed it among all but the youngest two. She then milked the cow and managed to throw it some hay from the loft. Work over, she huddled the children round the smouldering peat fire for warmth and when night came again she put the little ones to bed and sang them to sleep. Another day came and went with Agnes attending to the cow and dividing the dwindling stock of potatoes and oatmeal between her brothers and sisters. On the morning of the fourth day the blizzard died down and, telling the younger ones to keep by the fire, Agnes managed to stagger through the snow drifts to the next farm. The news spread quickly and within a short time a large search party was combing the fells. For over three days they floundered through deep snow, digging under boulders and searching every likely place of shelter, but without success. Dogs were brought in to help and soon the body of George Green was found, lying at the foot of a precipice. Some distance from the top of the precipice the searchers discovered Sarah's body, wrapped in her husband's overcoat. The signs indicated that the wife had collapsed with exhaustion and George Green, having covered her with his overcoat, had gone ahead, perhaps to try and get help or discover where he was and, staggering through the blizzard, had fallen over the rocky crag.

William Wordsworth organized a relief fund for the orphans and raised about £500 from sources all over the country, including the Queen and three of her daughters. The children were adopted or taken on as servants by families in the district. Wordsworth and his wife, Mary, accepted responsibility for Sally, but they were later to regret the decision. One day when she was looking after little Kate Wordsworth, she let her crawl about the kitchen floor. Rummaging through a heap of vegetables, Kate swallowed a lot of raw carrot and became violently ill and later died.

Peter found me and we had lunch in a café. Newspapers throughout Cumbria had given the Ravenglass book a marvellous write up and Peter had managed to collect quite a number of orders on the strength of it. After he had left, to visit booksellers in Windermere, I bought a newspaper and found a quiet bench in Borrans Park. Persistent heavy showers scattered groups of hikers, but I was snug and dry beneath the broad foliage of a large sycamore. In the mid afternoon a warm sun broke through and succeeded in driving the rain clouds over the great dome of Fairfield and swirling streamers of steam drifted over the fields as the heat penetrated the wet grass. I soaked up the sun until a vast swarm of greenfly descended from the sycamore and pestered me until I could stand it no longer. I ran for the bus station and my friendly Bedford back to Patterdale.

It was only when I was back at my tent I realized how much I had missed being with the ponies, even for such a short time. They were flat out in the sun, but came trotting over when I called. Thor still had the short dry cough, as though he had an irritating tickle in his throat, but it did not stop him nipping Jewel playfully and bounding round the field as they chased each other.

Having had a meal with Peter, I was not hungry. My stomach was conditioned to frugal living and I found that two meals were quite adequate to keep me fit. The fells looked superb as I wandered slowly along the path by the farm. Every rock stood out sharp in the air, washed clean by the rain. Finding myself close to Patterdale village I called at the White Lion for a glass of beer. I got talking to a couple of old chaps who told me they had once worked in Greenside Mine and had lived in Patterdale all their lives, and their grandfathers and great-grandfathers before them. They were a fund of tales about Patterdale in days gone by, and one said his grandfather often used to talk about a character called Michael Mattinson, who used to bring mail over Kirkstone Pass to the Kings Arms (now the Patterdale Hotel). He drove a cart with a horse in the shafts and a donkey as a leader. Every time they reached a pub the donkey would stop and refuse to budge until old Mattinson had bought him a drink.

I left them arguing about mining and went out into the cool evening. They were a grand old pair, belonging to a rapidly disappearing generation, who took great pride in their work and lived by rigid standards of courtesy and self-respect, which regrettably are dying with them.

The sky was ablaze with stars as I walked back to the farm and in the half-light the fells seemed twice as large as they closed in on the valley. Nearing my campsite, I was horrified to hear radios blaring into the night from several caravanettes which had arrived while I was away. I crawled into my sleeping-bag, but it was hours before the BBC switched off their transmitters and allowed me to go to sleep.

I woke early and went to have a look at Thor. The cough

seemed to have left him, but another day's rest would not do him any harm, so I went back to the tent to make breakfast. A blackbird was chirping merrily from an oak tree, but he was no match for the dawn chorus of transistors from the caravanettes, so he gave up and left. No one noticed. Filling a small rucksack with camera, binoculars, waterproofs and a few biscuits, I set off to walk the three miles or so along the main road to Aira Force. I was going to visit a great lover, or at least the ghost of one.

In a rocky, tree-lined gorge between Glencoyne Park and Gowbarrow Park, on the north side of Ullswater, Aira Beck descends in a series of imposing waterfalls. According to legend, Emma, a beautiful lady who lived nearby, was betrothed to one Sir Eglamore, but when her lover had not returned after a long absence, it affected her health and she took to wandering in her sleep. Sir Eglamore eventually returned and found Emma plucking twigs from the trees and throwing them into the beck to be carried down the Force. He watched for a while, not knowing she was asleep, then touched her. She woke suddenly and seeing him, shrieked with fright and fell over the steep cliff into the water. The knight jumped in after her, but it was too late. Heartbroken, Eglamore built a cell on the edge of the fall and lived there in solitude for many years. Poor Eglamore, when I arrived at the falls his vigil was being disturbed by hundreds of tourists, pouring from the car park. Swollen with rainwater, the falls were very impressive. Roaring torrents, sepia brown with peat carried down from the fells, boiled down the deep gorge, cascading with tremendous leaps into pools forty or fifty feet below. It would have been nice to have sat and thought about Emma and Sir Eglamore, but several coachloads of visitors arrived and the place was so crowded I climbed above the falls and on to the open fell of Gowbarrow Park. The sky was overcast and it was warm and muggy, with a thick haze over Ullswater. Across the lake

I hoped to see the path I wanted to take the next day, from Patterdale to Howtown, but the visibility was so poor I could barely make it out.

It was in this part of the Lake District that William Wordsworth wrote a few lines which were to cause much suffering to schoolboys, who like me, could never remember who wrote what, when it came to exam time. I have never been a fan of Wordsworth, since the day I was forced to miss my début in the school football team and stay behind and learn, parrot fashion:

> I wandered lonely as a cloud,
> That floats on high o'er vales and hills,
> When all at once I saw a crowd,
> A host of golden daffodils.
> Beside the lake, beneath the trees,
> Fluttering and dancing in the breeze.

Black clouds were advancing from the south as I hurried down the fell and I had just got my hands round a mug of hot tea, in the café by Aira Force car park, when there was a loud clap of thunder and torrential rain swept the valley. Within seconds, the almost deserted café was crowded with shivering people, dripping pools of water onto the floor from sodden clothing. There was no sign of the rain easing, so I pulled on my waterproof trousers and, with anorak hood tied firmly, splashed my way back along the road to Patterdale. On the roadside between Glenridding and Patterdale, I was attracted by what appeared to be a horse trough, protected by an ornate canopy with a slate roof. There was no plate or inscription saying why it was there, so I called at Patterdale Vicarage to ask the vicar if he knew. I was welcomed by the Reverend John Rogers, a large, hearty man, who bustled with enthusiasm and humour. Filling me with tea and biscuits, he explained that the ornate trough had served a much higher purpose than satisfying equine thirst, and, in fact, was a well that St Patrick himself had used, to baptize the locals. Apparently, that well-known Irishman had passed that way in AD 540 and built a church. Ever after, the place was called St Patrick's Dale, later abbreviated to Patterdale.

While I made a hole in his stock of shortbread biscuits, Mr Rogers recalled a number of tales about Patterdale in the old days. Brimming with laughter, he told the story of a one-time vicar of the parish, who was a hunting fanatic and spent so much time following the hounds, on the Sabbath he would say a quick blessing, then shoot off after the hunt. One Sunday, the hounds were in full cry by Hartsop, when the vicar spotted the bishop's carriage descending Kirkstone Pass. Bellowing to the hunt to follow him, they raced back to Patterdale and poured into the church, hounds and all. Disturbing rumours had reached the bishop about the devotion to duty of his incumbent and he was on his way to catch him out, but when his lordship quietly opened the church door, he saw the congregation kneeling and the vicar deep in prayer. Obviously the rumours were unfounded. Nodding approvingly, he climbed back into his carriage and continued on his way to Penrith. What he did not know was that the congregation were kneeling, not in prayer, but to hold the hounds down on the floor. As soon as the carriage had gone they rushed out again, in pursuit of the fox.

Glancing at a clock on the wall, I was amazed to find I had been in the vicarage for close on two hours and it was with great reluctance I eventually dragged myself away. I was hoping to leave the next day and there were one or two repair jobs to do on the pack-saddle. It was still raining when I reached the campsite and the field was a quagmire, churned up by the coming and going of the vehicles. While I checked through the waterlogged harness an amusing incident helped to dispel the gloom brought on by the weather. The caravanettes had a large tent attached to the side of each vehicle and, for some reason, they had all parked close together on a fairly steep grass slope. The owner of a van in the middle of the group either decided he did not like the company or he was going to the pub, and suddenly drove away. Unfortunately for his neighbour, the guy rope of his tent was hooked round the van's bumper bar and, although the driver jammed on his brakes, the van slid on down the wet grass. The rope came taut and there was a loud 'ping' as the press studs holding the canvas to the van parted and the tent fell away to reveal a large-busted lady, wearing nothing but a wedding ring, busily having a wash. She let out a piercing shriek and struggled to get into the van, but the door jammed. Finally, in desperation, she dived under the canvas of the fallen tent and crouched, as she thought, covered, but she had not gone far enough and a huge bottom protruded from under the tent. Her frantic husband rushed round not knowing what to do, until a kind neighbour hung a large bath towel over the exposed rear end and the panic was over. My sides ached so much from laughing I could hardly eat my dinner.

As the sun sank behind Helvellyn, the sky was a deep red and, if the old weather portent proved to be right, I would be as delighted as the shepherds.

CHAPTER 7

Martindale

The chirpy blackbird and I were the only ones who watched the dawn sun creep down the fellside and scoop up the cottonwool mist lying on the lake. It was one of those incredibly beautiful mornings which linger in the memory and make one forget the awful weather the Lake District can throw down when the mood takes it. The rich tones of the brown fells contrasted with the vivid green of the patchwork meadows, interwoven with strips of grey stone walls. Around the shore of the silent lake, gnarled branches of ancient oaks spread dark shadows over the water, providing a hiding-place for hungry trout to leap at unsuspecting flies. The ponies stood, transfixed, in the field, as though turned to stone and there was not a sound to be heard, save the musical blackbird, heralding a new day. From the caravanettes a discordant chorus chanted 'Radio One' and the spell was broken.

Thor and Jewel trotted over when I called and I checked their shoes before sending up a cloud of dust with a grooming brush and sorting tangled manes and tails. There was no sign of Thor's cough and I was deeply grateful to the Taylforths for letting us stay and rest. By nine o'clock I was loaded and leading the ponies out of the campsite and onto the ancient bridleway.

Long before a motor road was blasted through the rocks on the north side of Ullswater, the pack-horse road running along the side of Place Fell to Howtown, was the main route from Patterdale to Penrith. At fair times, strings of pack-horses came over the fells, with bells ringing, laden with all manner of goods for sale to the eager dalesfolk.

Occasionally, sheep and herds of Highland cattle would join the throng and when the far-travelled animals showed signs of fatigue one of the drovers would revive them by marching in front playing a lively air on the bagpipes. The drovers and their pipes had long gone to rest, and it was over a hundred years since Patterdale last held a fair, but the old path still existed, solidly built and paved with blocks of weathered stone.

From Side Farm it climbed gently up to a col between Silver Crag and the boulder-strewn slopes of Hare Shaw, and I let the ponies rest for a few minutes while I drank in the superb scenery. Beyond Silver Crag, the path plunged steeply down to the shore of Ullswater and wound among the trees before climbing again, above the wood, to a rocky platform and a breathtaking view across the lake to the deep gorge of Aira Force. Ahead, the path narrowed as it crossed the steep slope of scree and I waited until a line of walkers had reached my perch. As each one arrived I passed the time of day and was almost hoarse by the time the last one arrived.

'You may as well save your breath, mate,' he gasped as he stretched himself on the grass, 'There's another hundred and fifty behind me.' Looking along the path I saw what appeared to be a long line of Chinese coolies, carrying packs, advancing from the direction of Howtown.

'Hell's bells!' I exclaimed, 'where's all this lot come from?'

'Don't look so worried,' said the man, with an amused chuckle, 'we're not invading Cumberland, it's a Holiday Fellowship outing and we all met at Howtown to walk to Patterdale.'

An hour passed before the tail end reached us, but the ponies had a grand time, revelling in the attention of the cheerful group and crunching lumps of chocolate held out at arm's length by timid ladies. Thermos flasks and plastic sandwich boxes stowed away, the party departed, pouring towards Patterdale like a swarm of locusts.

Losing the shelter of the trees, the full heat of the sun burnt down from a cloudless sky and we were soon lathered with sweat as we crossed the unprotected fell. Skirting the corner of a wood, the path twisted down to a narrow footbridge crossing Scalehow Beck. Alarmed by the hollow sound of the bridge, Thor put one cautious hoof forward, then leapt back as if he had been stung.

'Get on, you daft idiot!' I yelled at him, but each time he shied away and gave a great display of bucking and rearing. Jewel sniffed at the planks, then hurried away to hide behind Thor. The bridge, though narrow, was quite strong and I jumped up and down in the middle of it to convince them it was safe, but they were not impressed. A packet of Polo mints and Jewel's sweet tooth eventually got us across. The crackle of paper brought her trotting to me and, mint by mint, I coaxed her on to the bridge, and before she realized it she was over and sucking the empty packet. Seeing Jewel on the opposite side of the beck, Thor raced frantically up and down the bank, but in the end he realized there was only one way and, closing his eyes, he thundered across the bridge to join us. The path widened, a little way ahead, but was so deeply rutted with the passage of farm vehicles, we were forced to climb onto the firm turf above it. Emerging onto the Sandwick to Howtown road, the ponies were unhappy as the streams of cars hooted their way past us, so finding a short cut on the map, we crossed Boardale Beck and followed an attractive little lane, overhung with sweet-scented hawthorn blossom and paved with a carpet of soft grass. The sight of all that lovely food at her feet was too much for Jewel and she almost dragged my arm off, trying to snatch mouthfuls, as I heaved her up the lane and through a farmyard at the foot of the steep-sided valley of Martindale.

From the farm, the bridlepath followed a stone wall,

separating fields from the open fell and the clink of the ponies' shoes striking against a rock was the only sound as they plodded mechanically on. Dozing in the saddle, I did not notice we were approaching a cottage until I was jerked to my senses by the frenzied yapping of two over-fed spaniels charging towards us. Lethargic in the heat, the ponies ignored them as they snapped at their heels, but the yappiest of the pair pushed his luck too far, and almost without missing a stride, Thor's broad hind foot catapulted the brute, still yapping, clean over the wall. Finding himself alone, the survivor beat a hasty retreat to the safety of the cottage and as we passed the door he was being consoled by a severe-looking matron, crooning, 'There, there now, have the nasty horses frightened you then.' I urged the ponies on faster, before she started looking for his mate.

Joining the dale road at Winter Crag Farm, a clanking sound behind me signalled a loose shoe on Jewel, but we kept going, following the narrow, winding road to its end at Dale Head Farm. Tom Mounsey, the farmer, and his son Brian, watched curiously as I rode into the yard, but they were very friendly and showed me a spot alongside a beck where I thankfully pitched camp and turned the ponies loose to roll in the soft dust of the track.

It was a gorgeous evening and a rare treat to sit outside the tent and drink a last mug of coffee before turning in. There was a Fell pony stallion in an adjoining field and he and Thor charged up and down, whinnying challenges at one another while Jewel looked on, bright eyed hoping to see a fight. I slept sounder, knowing a stout wall kept them apart.

The sound of the beck gurgling past the tent woke me as the first shafts of golden sunlight broke through the morning mists. I opened the tent door and retreated deeper into my sleeping-bag as the sharp mountain air flowed in and dispersed the warm fug. Behind the farmhouse the 'pee-wit' of the lapwings sounded across the still valley and, in a field below the tent, lambs rose stiffly on spindly legs, shaking the dew off their backs in a cloud of spray. As the sun crept higher and warmed the air, silver mists rose, swirling about the tree tops, before floating high above the valley to join the fleecy clouds. I had breakfast in the sun and, as the primus roared, the smell of frying bacon and coffee put such a keen edge on my appetite I could hardly wait until it was ready.

I had never been to Martindale before and was particularly keen to explore the Nab, a steep-sided, conical fell, rising above the farm and dividing the head of the dale into the valleys of Bannerdale and Rampsgill. Tom said it would be all right to stay another night and also gave me permission to go on the Nab, one of the few fells in the Lake District where there is no public right of way.

I called the ponies over and tied Jewel to a tree while I banged the nails tight in her loose shoe. Both of them gleamed with health and bounded away like a pair of foals when I had finished inspecting their feet and backs. When I first talked about my journey a local 'expert', who liked to air her superior knowledge, yet was never seen actually sitting on a horse, was sneeringly critical of my plans and insisted that the ponies would never survive on less than three feeds of oats a day. I pointed out that the work-horses of the Argentine ranchers and American cowpunchers were not pampered in such a way, but she would not listen.

'But my deah,' she crowed, 'those people are peasants and can hardly be expected to know better.'

Heaven preserve the noble horse from such stupid ignorance!

By ten o'clock the sun had really got its boiler stoked up and the inside of the tent was like an oven. I had brought a pair of shorts with me, but had so despaired of it ever being warm enough to wear them, they had been used for all sorts of purposes, from mopping up spilt paraffin to cleaning the tack. I dug the smelly bundle out of the tent bag and, with shirt and anorak tied round my waist, strode across the fields to the stalkers' path up the Nab. It was great to feel the sun burning into my skin and the freedom of the shorts enabled me to pound up the fell at a cracking pace. In the days when deer stalking in Martindale was an essential part of the social calendar for the London gentry, a path had been cut right across the face of the Nab, so that trophies could be brought down by pony. The path petered out just below the summit and a wilderness of peat hags stretched across the broad plateau towards Rest Dodd and the long ridge of High Street. This was the home of the only remaining open country herd of Red Deer in the Lake District, and I moved carefully, hoping for a glimpse of them. Crawling through the cool peat, I peered cautiously over the edge into Rampsgill and there they were. I counted twenty hinds and five stags and as those majestic animals moved effortlessly over the ground, with antlers held high, I was struck with a dreadful pang of remorse, remembering the time when, as a deer stalker with the Forestry Commission in Inverness-shire, I was paid to slaughter them. They swarmed in their thousands in the remote glens of Scotland and, in wintertime, when the snow piled up against the fences, they jumped into the forest and wreaked havoc among young trees. I shot ten or twelve a day for months, and became so sick of the carnage, one bright sunny morning, having shot a fawn, mistaking it for a roe deer, as it desperately tried to escape, I walked down the glen to the forester's office, laid my rifle on his desk and resigned.

As I watched, the deer were obviously uneasy, darting forward a few yards to snatch a mouthful or two before moving on in little groups. It is a fact that deer seldom look uphill and I was able to wriggle almost to within two hundred yards of them before they winded me. A big stag shot to his feet and was away like a flash, the rest streaming after him, leaping across ditches like miniature steeple-chasers. They poured like a brown tide, through a gap in the wall and within seconds they had vanished. A buzzard circled overhead, but there would be no steaming gralloch for him this day.

Walking back to the summit, I sat on a rock and looked down on Martindale. Far below, the freshly whitewashed buildings of Dale Head Farm stood out bright against the fellside. By the house an alien blob of orange marked the position of my tent. On the Rampsgill side of the valley was a rather odd collection of buildings with red roofs, marked on the map as 'The Bungalow'. I learnt later that it was once a shooting-lodge used by the 'yellow earl' or to give him his full title, the fifth Earl of Lonsdale. A great sportsman, he would descend on the valley with a bevy of pals, during the stalking season, for a month of high jinks and deer stalking. Dale Head Farm once had a veranda along the front, where the ladies and their maids watched while the men folk sat on the Nab, blasting away at the deer. In 1895, the Earl entertained no less a person than Kaiser Wilhelm, at The Bungalow. Perhaps it was here that the ambitious Prussian developed such a love for the Lake District that, nineteen years later, he tried to steal it for himself.

The view along the valley to Ullswater was obscured by a thick haze, so I retraced my steps down the pony track to the farm. Reaching the tent, I stretched out on the grass and, as if at a signal, a thick bank of cloud blotted out the sun and the air turned so chilly I was soon out of the shorts and pulling on thick trousers and a woolly sweater. A blustery wind bounced off the fells and rattled the tent with such violent gusts I gathered large stones and piled them on the tent pegs and around the sides. An evil-looking, coal-black cloud swirled over High Street and crept down the Nab like a flow of liquid ebony. For a day or so we had basked in the Lake

District weather of the picture postcards, but now the gods were mixing a special Cumberland brew that would have even the most exuberant envoys of the tourist board choking on their superlatives.

As he stumbled past the tent, hurrying for the shelter of the farm buildings, Thor let out a long rasping cough and my heart missed a beat. He had been fine since we left Patterdale and now, for no accountable reason, it was back again. I lay in my sleeping-bag, worried sick about him, as the wind roared down off the fell tops like an express train.

A howling gale raged all night and sleep was impossible. Wave after wave of driving rain lashed into the tent, the hysterical wind howled with fury, as it clawed the fragile canvas. The noise was deafening and, fearing that the tent would be torn to pieces, I lit a candle and got dressed. Packing what gear I could into the kit-bags, I lay on them, and, gripping a torch ready for a fast escape, worked out the quickest route to Tom Mounsey's barn. At four o'clock the wind dropped to a breeze and the rain stopped. I could hear Thor coughing his heart out and as soon as it was light I went out to look at him. Jewel stood by with a worried expression, wanting to help, but not knowing what to do. I was not too sure myself, and could only stand helplessly as his whole body shook with the spasms.

'The big feller sounds in bad fettle,' said Tom, suddenly appearing at my side.

'Aye, you're right, Tom,' I replied, 'if only I could get him something for that cough. It's getting worse.'

'That's nay problem,' continued Tom, 'I'll get Brian to run you into Penrith.'

His son cheerfully got the car out and, within an hour, I was explaining Thor's symptoms to a vet. Rummaging through the dispensary cupboards he produced a bottle of penicillin, to be injected once a day, and enough Berkfurin powders to be given three times a day for a week. I winced as I handed over £7, but it was essential to nip the cough in the bud, or the whole trip would be in jeopardy. Back at Dalehead, Tom gave me a small bag of flaked maize to mix with the powders and, while Thor's nose was in the bucket, I whacked the hypodermic needle into his neck. As a precaution, I gave Jewel a powder, but even when it was mixed with flaked maize, she did not like the taste and kept spitting it out. A thick layer of honey did the trick and when I turned them loose she followed Thor into the field, pulling weird faces as she tried to lick the gluey mess off her nose.

Not having had any sleep the previous night, my eyelids felt like lumps of lead and by seven o'clock I was in my sleeping-bag. The gusty wind returned and tugged at the flysheet, but the rain kept off and I slept undisturbed.

CHAPTER 8

Along High Street

I woke early and stuck my head out of the tent to look at the weather. The wind was still blowing, but, glory be, there was not a cloud in the sky and a cautious sun peered over the rim of the valley as if wondering whether it dare climb higher. Gulping down a hurried breakfast, I gave Thor his medicine and, having loaded Jewel, went to the farmhouse to thank Tom Mounsey. He would not take a penny for his help and, as I rode away, I could not help thinking that if there were more like him the world would be a better place.

The vet advised me not to over-exert Thor, so I let him meander at his own lumbering pace as we climbed diagonally up Beda Fell. It was a fine, clear morning, but the higher we climbed, the stronger the wind became, and, reaching the top of the path, on a ridge overlooking the deep cleft of Boardale, it was so fierce I could hardly stay in the saddle. The pack developed an ominous list, so I pulled the ponies under the shelter of a rocky knoll to adjust the bags and girths. It was grand to escape the ceaseless buffeting of the wind and it gave me a chance to appreciate the view. Beyond Patterdale, the thin line of the old pack-horse road to Grasmere stood out plainly as it followed Grisedale Beck up the long valley, before climbing slowly to Grisedale Tarn, nestling in a hollow between the crumbling sides of Dollywaggon Pike and Fairfield, a welcome resting-place for the teams of pack-ponies before continuing on the winding descent down by Little Tongue Gill. The Helvellyn ridge was crystal clear, with the concrete trig point on the summit shining like an ivory icon, urging on the droves of brightly-clad pilgrims, spread out along the sharp rocks of

Striding Edge. A short distance below my view-point, the paths from Patterdale, Boardale and Martindale converged like the spokes of a wheel on a rectangle of stones almost hidden in the thick grass. With each of the valleys having its own church, with a history reaching back many centuries, it seems odd that a chapel should be built high on a fell top, but that is what the ruin is reputed to have been. Perhaps it was the meeting-place of a persecuted minority, who gathered to worship where, in those times, few dared to venture. Whatever their particular brand of religion, to toil up this wild part of the fells on a bleak winter's day would have taken a lot of faith and many a present-day clergyman, surveying the rows of empty pews on a Sunday morning, must wish that his parishioners possessed the same fervour.

The wind was waiting for us when we emerged from our shelter and the ponies staggered as repeated gusts drove into them like a battering-ram. Keeping well away from the edge of the crags overlooking Martindale, I pitched forward into the gale, Thor's reins wrapped tightly round my wrist, as he floundered, half-blinded, behind me. At Angle Tarn, miniature water spouts whipped the surface into a foaming mass, showering us with icy water as we crept by. The path alongside the tarn was very wet and boggy in places, and we had to make numerous long detours. Exhausted and gasping for breath, I sheltered behind a small crag and lay against a boulder, aching in every muscle. Cheated of its sadistic sport, the wind howled angrily overhead, but for the moment we had escaped. I was breaking up a bar of barley sugar for Thor and Jewel when the most remarkable sight appeared from the direction of Patterdale. Two hefty chaps staggered along the path, carrying an enormous holdall between them, crammed to bursting point with cans of ale. Some distance behind, a poor little fellow puffed and sweated under the weight of a large assortment of fishing-rods, landing-nets and folding stools. As each gust of wind whacked against all this paraphernalia, it spun him round like a weather vane and he pirouetted along the edge of the tarn as if in a scene from Swan Lake. He ended the performance by falling over his resting mates and knocking the bag of booze into the water. A tirade of colourful expletives, delivered in a broad Lancashire accent, warmed the air and left no one in any doubt what they thought of their overloaded friend.

They were downing their fifth can of McEwans and gaily flinging their empties into the tarn, by the time we had ploughed our way up past Satura Crag to a gate in a wall. Fortunately it was wide enough to accommodate the width of the path, but on the other side the path deteriorated rapidly, and finally sank into a most horrible looking bog. Blasting across the open fellside, the wind was merciless, and I could scarcely stay on my feet as I searched for a way round the sea of oozing peat. Leaving the ponies tied together, I went ahead to reconnoitre a route and had hardly gone a few steps, when a bird flew out of the grass under Thor's nose. He bolted like a black arrow and, when Jewel's lead rope became taut, he continued minus saddle. It was the Wasdale incident all over again, only this time we were on open fell in the teeth of a gale, without a scrap of shelter anywhere. I cursed the great fool until his ears singed, as I chased after the fleeing saddle blanket. Hauling the saddle out of the slime, I discovered the girth straps had parted again and both buckles had been torn off. It was hopeless attempting to go on until it was repaired, so out came the mending gear, and with the wind doing its damndest to blow me back to Martindale, I sat on the wet hillside, anorak zipped up tight and woollen balaclava pulled down over my face, trying to thread a needle with frozen fingers. Saddlers' needles have very small eyes and, having chewed the thread to a fine point, I would get it almost through and the wind would blow it out again. I managed it at last, and with chattering teeth,

The author making his pack-saddle.

Jewel carrying the completed saddle.

The ponies securely
hobbled after the
return trip over Black
Sail Pass.

What a relief! Thor
enjoying a roll in the
grass at the end of a
hard day.

Crossing the ford at
Gatesgarth,
Buttermere.

Weatherbound at
Gatesgarth, the
author updates his log.

Pack-saddle problems on Sticks Pass.

Four-hoof drive truimphs—a stranded Jeep on Garburn Pass.

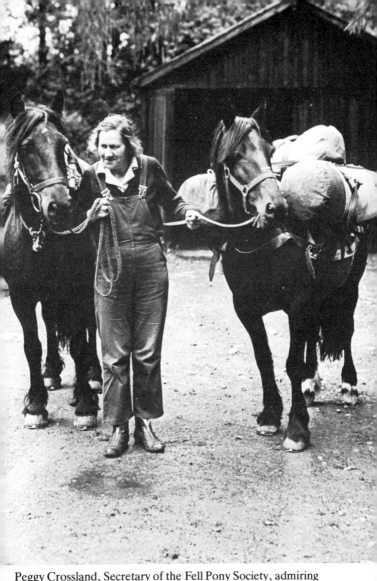

Peggy Crossland, Secretary of the Fell Pony Society, admiring
Thor and Jewel.

Jewel weighed down
by the pack-saddle
sinks into a bog.

Fortunately after
several hours she
manages to stagger to
her feet again.

Campsite at Patterdale, overlooking Ullswater.

Pillar Rock from Gillerthwaite campsite.

The never-ending chore of mending tack.

The journey over, author and ponies arrive home.

painfully pieced the bits together. As I worked away a party of elderly walkers appeared over the hill and, as each one passed by, I was greeted with a polite 'Good afternoon', as though there was nothing out of the ordinary in a strange figure, red balaclava pulled down over face, sitting on a fellside in a gale, calmly sewing. It was so ridiculous I started to laugh, but the party quickened their pace and disappeared over a rise without looking back.

I was frozen to the marrow by the time the saddle was buckled over Thor's broad back. Throwing caution to the wind, I led them straight across the bog and with more luck than judgement, finally scrambled onto the rocky path leading up to the Knott, a rocky, fortress-shaped mound, overlooking the reservoir of Hayeswater. At the Mountain Rescue Box near the top of the Knott, we had a few moments of welcome relief from the wind, and actually sweated in the heat of the sun. Without the wind it would have been a gorgeous day, but on the exposed ridge between Riggindale and Hayeswater, the sweat soon dried off as the gale found us again.

The broad flat plateau which marks the highest point of the long ridge running down the eastern side of the Lake District, between Troutbeck in the south and Tirril in the north, has probably played a more important part in Lakeland history than any other fell. When the Romans pushed their road from Ravenglass to Ambleside, then north, to Brougham, near Penrith, the ridge was a natural highway, safe from the dangers of the thickly wooded valleys. It was originally known as Brettestrete (the road of the Britons) but over the years, it has changed to High Street. The wide summit was a great meeting-place in the days when shepherds used to get together once a year, to return strayed sheep. Instead of shoving them in the back of a Landrover, like they do today, it was an opportunity for a social occasion, and the tenth of July was a day eagerly looked forward to in the farming calendar. When the serious business of swopping sheep was over, a dinner was laid out, with plenty of ale to drink, rolled up the fellside in barrels by the local lads. After a meal there was fox-hunting and a lively sports, held with prizes for wrestling, jumping and running, but the main attraction of the day was horse-racing. Instead of galloping, the riders had to keep to a trot or they were disqualified, and, at a height of 2,719 feet above sea-level, it must sure have been the highest racecourse in Britain.

The roof of High Street was deserted as we battled through the storm to the summit cairn. My watch showed it was time for Thor's medicine, but it was no day for lingering and he would have to wait until we reached the valley. A thick bank of grey cloud poured over Mardale Ill Bell and dropped down Blea Water Crag, only to be caught by a fierce updraught and flung skywards in a boiling mass, like steam rising from a giant cauldron. The stream was, in turn, gripped by the wind and hurled across High Street to tumble into Hayeswater Gill. Visibility was reduced to a few yards, but the wind did not let up for a second. Thor's broad belly provided enough shelter for me to work out a compass course for Thornthwaite Crag and, compass in one hand and reins in the other, I lurched forward again, until the tall stone obelisk on Thornthwaite loomed ahead and guided me towards the Troutbeck valley. Following a broken path, we suddenly walked out of the cloud into bright sunshine and it was a huge relief to be able to see the valley below. Without warning, the wind died and I had become so accustomed to leaning into it I almost fell flat on my face. It was like crossing into another world. One minute we were being battered and frozen by a gale and the next we were in a land of green grass and warm sunshine, with skylarks overhead, singing their hearts out. The change was so abrupt I wondered if it was an hallucination, but hallucination or not, the ponies lost no time in tearing into the grass and while they grazed, I lay back and let the sun melt the icicles in my veins.

The Roman road slants down the side of Froswick, easily at first, then steepens without warning, on very smooth grass. I was leading the ponies warily down an awkward section, when the pack shifted and knocked Jewel off balance. Her hind legs slipped forward and, rooted to the spot, I watched her, unable to help, as she slid towards the edge. Teetering on the brink of a long drop into the valley, she somehow managed to get a grip and fell into the hillside. Had she gone the other way the world would have ended for brave Jewel. My heart missed several beats as she struggled to her feet, but she seemed none the worse for the ordeal. Safely off the fell, I checked her for any signs of injury, but apart from a green streak down a flank, where she had slid down the grass, there was not a mark on her. I could not believe my luck and I celebrated by sharing a bar of chocolate among the three of us.

Along the valley, the path was firm and level and I relaxed in the saddle, enjoying the pleasant ride, as Thor made his own way. Trapped by the steep sides of the fells, the heat was intense and I peeled off down to a tee-shirt as we plodded on. We passed several tempting sites where I could have pitched camp, but I wanted to get permission first and we continued on till we came to a farm. I was not too happy when I saw the National Trust sign over the door, but, although the farmer no doubt had instructions not to allow camping, he could see that with two ponies I would hardly be welcomed on the large complex of tents and caravans farther down the valley and he said it would be all right for one night. In a quiet spot by the side of Hagg Beck I pitched camp. As I unfolded the tent a Martindale spider crawled out and inspected the campsite. He must have scratched his head, wondering where he was and, by the time he had walked back home, his eight hairy legs would be drooping at the kneecaps.

Within a short time a thick chunk of Cumberland sausage was sizzling in the pan, with two eggs and a few potatoes to keep it company. The ponies were lying flat out in the evening sun and, after I had eaten, I took a mug of coffee and sat with them. Thor had not coughed all day and as I rested against his massive frame he breathed easily, without a trace of the awful rasping sound that had rumbled out of him in Martindale. Later, I mixed his medicine with a little flaked maize and, giving Jewel a taste to stop her feeling jealous, I left them nibbling the sweet grass. As darkness fell a full moon hung like a solitary pearl over the peaceful valley, and, lulled by the murmur of the beck, I fell into a dreamless sleep.

CHAPTER 9

Delay in Kentmere

Next morning I woke to the sound of rain pattering on the canvas and Thor coughing as badly as ever. I could not believe it. Last night the sky had been crystal clear, with not a cloud to be seen, and old Thor never uttered as much as a wheeze. Now we were back to square one again. Life was becoming a game of snakes and ladders.

I gave Thor his medicine and injected a dose of penicillin into his neck. He looked utterly fed up and dejected as the rain dripped off the end of his nose and I was becoming increasingly worried about this peculiar malady which appeared to come and go at any time.

The rain stopped as I made breakfast and the clouds rolled away to reveal the sun, climbing slowly into a deep blue sky. The undulating ridge of Ill Bell and Froswick stood out sharply as it rose in a long sweep to Thornthwaite Crag at the head of the valley. While the sun dried the dew off the tent, I lingered over a mug of coffee and watched a kestrel work methodically back and forward across the fellside, searching for breakfast. Zooming effortlessly about, it would brake sharply and hover, waiting for an unsuspecting shrew to come hurrying through the grass, then plunge like an arrow onto its prey.

It was approaching eleven o'clock as I walked the ponies out of the field and down the track towards Long Green Head Farm. In the fields behind the crumbling walls, a vast carpet of sunlit buttercups almost covered the green sward and reached high up the fellside to merge with the new bracken. Hawthorn trees, dotted here and there along the track, were ablaze with fresh blossom and as we passed each one a delicate fragrance hung around it in an invisible cloud. Through the farmyard the track rose steadily above the valley and sprawling complex of Limefitt Caravan Park, and at a gate, joined the Garburn Pass, at one time an important pack-horse route, connecting Troutbeck and Kentmere.

The name 'Garburn' is said to mean the 'muddy river' and the dark brown of the deeply-eroded, weather-gouged surface certainly gives the impression of a dried-up river bed. In the eighteenth century there were so many complaints about it from drovers, that the local magistrate made an order for the inhabitants of Kentmere and Applethwaite to repair the pass, because 'it is so utterly much out of repair and in decay that a great part of it is not passable for neither man nor horse to travel through the said ways without danger of being bogged in the moss or lamed among the stones and if not repaired before the next session the inhabitants of each place to be fined the sum of £10 severally'. If only present-day authorities would show the same concern for these rapidly deteriorating historical routes, but their consciences are seldom stirred beyond the state of the tarmac ribbon accessible to the motor car.

The pass climbed at an easy angle and all the way the view was magnificent, but poor Thor laboured so much I slackened his girth a few notches and led him to the top. At Garburn Nook the track levelled out and a ripple of a breeze danced through the hot air and brought a few seconds of welcome relief from the burning sun. Thor perked up a bit after a rest and Troutbeck gradually faded out of sight as the track descended towards the wooded slopes of Kentmere. We worked our way down a horrible mixture of loose boulders and wet hollows and, approaching a strange green object wedged in a patch of broken rock, I was astonished to discover it was a Jeep. What possessed its owner to think he could get a vehicle down a track difficult even for a walker, I could not imagine. The engine was still warm, but there was no one about, so I assumed he was either in Troutbeck or Kentmere, trying to persuade a farmer to haul it out with his tractor. Looking at the way the Jeep was wedged, it was plain that someone would have to dig deep down into his wallet before his pride and joy reached the road again.

Crossing Hall Gill the angle of the path eased off and the rock gave way to soft, springy turf. I pulled the ponies under the shade of a large silver birch and, while they plucked at the grass, I stretched out in the cool bracken. In the forest of stalks the insect world was in full swing. Massive dor beetles lumbered like tanks through the grass, sometimes falling over in their clumsiness and lying on their backs with flailing legs, until they managed to flip themselves upright. Ants heaved on twigs so large that, in comparison, it was like a man hauling a full-sized tree along with his teeth. More ants came along to assist and help heave the burden over rocks and dead bracken stalks towards the mound of their nest. They worked quickly and methodically, as if each one had an allotted task and with amazing efficiency each job was completed. There were no arguments, sit-down strikes, go slows or similar disputes invented by man. Everyone worked for the benefit of the community and, down there in the grass, was a message for the mortals above, whose supposedly superior intellect and technology are moving them unerringly towards total destruction.

A breeze swirled up from the valley and rustled through the leaves of the birch, but it was not strong enough to drive away the scores of flies swarming round the ponies' faces. Tails constantly swished to and fro, with frequent jingling of harness, as they shook themselves furiously in an attempt to dislodge the menace. A lone scout droned by and spotting me, called his pals over. I shot down the first attack with my cap, but with kamikaze defiance, the squadron reformed and swarmed at me in such numbers I was driven out of the shade into the sun.

The ancient pele tower of Kentmere Hall appeared through the trees as the track wound down towards the sprawling hamlet. Throughout the whole journey round the Lake District, I was always uneasy when I approached civilization, wondering what sort of reception I would get and whether I would find a place for the ponies. When I lived on the Isle of Lewis, in the Outer Hebrides, it was the custom for a traveller to call at any house and ask for shelter and it would never be refused. Returning to the mainland, I forgot that modern living had done away with the old courtesies and, one rainy day in a remote part of the country, I came to a house, and, knocking on the door, asked if I could shelter. I was brought forcibly back to reality when the owner, a retired Army colonel, told me to get the hell out of it or he would call the police. I suppose I was stupidly naïve, but that incident has stuck with me, and ever since then, large white houses give me the creeps. When I looked down at Kentmere it seemed to be full of them.

As we crept past an elegant, ivy-covered mansion, with a superb garden and ornate metal gate, an old lady wearing an enormous straw hat and looking, for all the world, like Beatrix Potter, watched us from behind a clump of azaleas. The only response to my polite 'Good afternoon' was a stony stare and when, further down the road, a man standing at the garden gate of another smart house, was dour and unhelpful, I began to think that Kentmere was as inhospitable as Watendlath.

The narrow road opened out into a small square, then curved round the side of a rather gloomy looking, cement-faced church, before descending a steep hill to the River Kent. On the bridge spanning the swift flowing river, I stared into the water, wondering how I was going to find a campsite and grazing for the ponies. I was watching a fat trout darting from rock to rock, as it made its way upstream, when a strange squeaking sound attracted my attention and round a bend in the road an old chap appeared on an ancient bicycle. He pedalled slowly, with just enough motion to keep the machine upright, and as the wheel turned, the long neglected bearings groaned a plea for oil. With a squeal of worn brake blocks, he pulled up level with me and, a fraction before the bike fell over, he put a foot to the ground.

'How's thee fettle?' he enquired, in a strong local accent.

'I'm fine, thanks,' I replied. 'Are there any farms in the valley that'd let me camp the night with the ponies?'

He thought for a moment, then said, 'Gerrard Hayton, at Brow Top would probably let you stay, but he's just gone down the road in his van.' Scratching his head under his cap, he continued, 'Mind you, his brother lives in the big house on the corner, I'll ask him when Gerrard'll be back.'

Climbing off the bike, he pushed it towards the swishest house in the valley, while I followed nervously in his wake. Leaning the bike on the wall, he leaned over the garden gate and called, 'Are you there, Leonard? There's a chap wants to know when Gerrard'll be back'.

A pleasant looking man emerged from a greenhouse and I stammered out my story about how I was travelling through the Lake District on horseback and was looking for a place to camp and graze the ponies and if he would direct me to his brother's farm I would be on my way and would not trouble him further. As I spoke, beads of sweat ran down my face, and it had nothing to do with the heat. Jewel had fixed her beady eyes on a rose bush growing on the side of the man's immaculate lawn and was edging slowly through the gate, with Thor only a tail's distance behind her. I was saved from being hounded out of the valley by the three children who rushed down from the house and made such a fuss of the ponies and fed them sweets, they forgot about the roses. Having listened to what I had to say, the man said there was no need for me to trail up to the farm, as he owned a field opposite the house and I was welcome to use it.

He led the way to a gate and a lovely sheltered meadow with a beck flowing through it, and plenty of fresh grass. It was a delightful campsite and, rid of saddles and harness, the ponies enjoyed a long, relaxing roll in the buttercups. I pitched the tent, but within minutes it was like an oven inside, so I sat in the shade of a wall waiting for the cool of evening before preparing a meal. The owner of the field joined me and we chatted for a while. He told me his name was Leonard Hayton and, although brought up in farming, he had qualified as a solicitor and was in practice in Windermere. As we talked, his wife appeared with a large container of water, to save me numerous trips to the house. I mixed lemonade crystals with it, but I was so dry I drank four or five mugs full before I could appreciate the taste. Mrs Hayton said that a vet was coming to look at a sick goat the next day, so I asked her to get him to look at Thor before he left.

Later in the evening Leonard invited me up to the house and in the magnificent, wood-lined lounge, with its great stone fireplace, I enjoyed the most interesting evening I had had for many a year. Leonard was a gifted poet who wrote in the Westmorland dialect and not only did he write, but he had a way of reading that brought a poem alive. Logs in the open hearth crackled and spat and the leaping flames cast flickering shadows on the ceiling as Leonard read poem after poem capturing the atmosphere of life on a dales farm and Lakeland in days gone by. It was long past midnight when I crawled, bleary-eyed, into the tent, but it was an evening I would not have missed for the world.

Thor's constant, racking cough disturbed me a lot during the night and when the heat of the sun beating through the canvas eventually woke me up, I realized I had slept late into the morning. I was eating breakfast when the vet arrived and I explained how, one day, Thor would be fine and the next he would cough his heart out. He took a long time over his examination, then staggered me by announcing that Thor had a touch of bronchitis and needed resting for a week. The vet departed, promising to drop some medicine off at Leonard's office in the afternoon.

It was a terrible blow and it seemed that the trip would have to be abandoned and Thor transported home. My dwindling funds would not stand another hefty vet's bill and the cost of staying in the Hayton's field for a week would finish it altogether. Feeling absolutely depressed, I sneaked away from the campsite and the laughter of the Hayton children, and, following a cart track, found myself on a crag high above Kentmere. It was a beautiful day, but even the magnificent view and the joyful song of the skylark did little to gladden my heart. On the other side of the valley, the path leading to Nan Bield Pass climbed tantalizingly up the fellside, before disappearing down to Haweswater, leaving me to bemoan my misfortune in not being able to follow it.

On the way back to the campsite, my head reeled with the effort of trying to find a way round having to abandon the journey. We had come a long way and endured a lot of hardship, since setting out from Ravenglass and to give up now was too awful to contemplate. Perhaps I could leave Thor in the Hayton's field and walk the rest of the way, taking Jewel to carry all my gear. The painful thought of leaving behind my best friend to fend for himself soon squashed that idea. Maybe the vet would be willing to wait until I got back to Ravenglass and searched for a job before paying his bill, and the Haytons might also agree to wait for whatever amount they wanted for allowing us to stay in their field for a week. The more I thought about it, the less attractive it became. Vets have a living to make, like anyone else, so why should he trust a perfect stranger to pay up when it suited him. As for asking the Haytons to wait, it would be throwing their kindness back in their face. I returned to the tent no nearer a solution that when I left it.

While I was busy cleaning the tack, Leonard's wife, Sandra, came into the field, clutching a large paper bag. She had called at the vet's on the way to collect the children from school and picked up Thor's medicine.

'Tony said to be sure and dose him regularly,' she warned, handing over the bulging packet. 'Oh,' she went on, remembering more instructions, 'don't use a hypodermic needle more than once.'

Tearing the bag open, I spread the contents on the grass and gulped at the sight of an expensive array of powders, bottles of penicillin, and a large plastic container of cough mixture. Thor's bronchial gremlins were in for a hard time when this lot swilled round their ankles, but the thought of what it was going to cost sent a shiver through me. Sandra broke through my thoughts.

'By the way, you've got to rest the pony for at least a week and Leonard said you've not to worry, you can stay as long as you like.' Overjoyed at their kindness, I was in a happier mood as I mixed the yellow powders with a handful of flaked maize, and dosed both Thor and Jewel. The instructions on the cough mixture said two tablespoonsful twice a day, but I did not fancy the idea of eating my porridge with my only spoon, after it had been used for pouring physic down horsy throats, so I hit on another idea. Using the hypodermic syringe I had got from the Penrith vet, I poured two tablespoonsful of cough mixture into it and marked the level. Pushing the syringe, minus the needle, into a pony's mouth, it was a marvellous way of squirting the dose down the throat. The mixture smelt quite pleasant and judging by the way they sniffed round the bottle for more it must have tasted all right. Jewel lost her enthusiasm for sharing Thor's medicine when I whacked the long needle into his neck and injected a dose of penicillin.

When Leonard came home he was very sympathetic about Thor's illness and assured me that we could stay until he was better. We talked well into the night and when I eventually tore myself away, I discovered it was pouring with rain. Thor's cough rang across the field, but I buried my head in my sleeping-bag and tried not to listen.

One of Thor's powders had to be given every three hours and, having got up twice during the night to stand shivering in the rain, I was shattered next morning. Heavy rain thumped on the fly-sheet and outside the usually placid beck running by the tent foamed and boiled as the water piled up against the wall, fighting to get through an overburdened drain. It was warm and cosy in the tent with the primus stove roaring away and after a leisurely breakfast I dosed the ponies and crept back into the warmth to read a book about Kentmere that Leonard had lent me. Despite the grim life, the inhabitants of the dale must have been a hardy lot in the old days. The book opened with the information that 'there died in Kentmere in Westmorland on the 17th October, 1780, Mr Martin Stevenson, in the 117th year of his age'. In a later chapter I came across the touching story of Mary Walker, the local postwoman; in 1892, as well as bringing up twelve children and caring for a blind husband, she walked the eight mile round trip to Stavely six days a week, to collect the mail bags, then delivered the post all along the dale. As if that was not enough for any mortal, as a sideline she taught sewing at the local school, cleaned the church and baked oatcakes for sale.

Browsing through the end of the book I discovered a Lakeland poet I had never heard of before. Overshadowed by the reputation of the Wordsworths and other hallowed names, Charles Williams, the poet of Kentmere, was almost unknown outside his native dale. Unlike the wealthy, comfortable existence enjoyed by the fashionable poets, Charles was the son of a struggling farmer. The locals had him doomed from the start, for on the day and at the hour he was born a huge stone rolled down Wallow Crag into Haweswater. The old sages muttered that it was a bad sign and meant that the boy was born to be drowned. As he grew it was obvious he was not cut out for farming and when the other boys were roughing each other up or raiding birds' nests, Charles would wander in the woods or lie in the grass, staring at the landscape. When he was sixteen he was walking over the fells one day, when he heard screams and racing in the direction of the cries, saw a young girl being chased by a bull. Running to her, he snatched an umbrella from her hand and unfurled it in the bull's face and drove it off. Charles took her home and, as the years rolled by, the friendship developed into love. He was twenty before he finally gathered enough courage to ask her to marry him and when she agreed he rushed home to pour his love onto paper.

> If all the world was made of kisses
> And all those kisses were made for me
> And I was made for you, my love
> How happy we should be.
> If all the graces were joined in one
> And all the wit and beauty too,
> They'd make a maid like you, my love,
> They'd make a maid like you.

Sadly, Maria was struck down by an illness the doctors could neither diagnose nor cure and she wasted away and died. Charles was so shattered with grief it affected his mind and one day, when he failed to return from a walk, a search party found him lying in Haweswater, in the very spot where the rock had rolled into the water, years before.

The tragic story of Charles Williams made me feel very gloomy, so I cheered the atmosphere by cranking up the stove and heating a pan of coffee. A nineteenth-century cobbler's bill in the back of the book was so hilariously naïve it soon helped to drive away the depression.

		£	s	d
Nov. 16th	To clogged up, Miss	0	2	
Dec. 14th	To mended up, Miss	1	3½	
Jan. 13th	To toe-topped, Master	0	3	
April 1st	To turned up, clogged up and mended, the Maid	1	7¾	
May 1st	To lined, bound and put a patch on, Madam	0	6	
May 10th	To soling, the Maid	0	8½	
May 14th	To topping, Madam	0	6	
May 15th	To putting a patch	0	2½	
May 16th	To stretching and easing, little, Master	0	2	
		£0	5	5¼

At midday it was still raining hard, but I felt so stiff through lack of exercise I pulled on my waterproofs and tramped up the cart track to the crag I had found the previous day. There was not much of a view, as I sheltered under an overhang and watched the rain sweeping across the fells, but somehow, even in saturation, the valley had a certain, patient beauty, which is difficult to define, yet is very much a part of the Lake District. In the lower valley thick cloud hung above the fresh green fields, almost touching the tops of the walls by a narrow sliver of water, once the great mere from which the valley takes its name. Years ago the valley fathers, in their wisdom, drained it to increase the amount of grazing land, but because the mills along the banks of the River Kent relied on the mere to keep the waterwheels turning in dry weather, a reservoir had to be built high in the fells where the source of the river spills from under Bleathwaite Crag.

A sudden change in the direction of the wind drove the rain into my sheltered niche so, bent almost double, I headed into the downpour and slithered through ankle-deep mud down a path to Kentmere Church and the road.

In the Hayton's field, the ponies stood like statues, backs to the wind in the shelter of the wall and never moved a muscle as I went through the routine of squirting cough mixture down their throats and injecting Thor with penicillin. Their ears felt warm and underneath the thick outer layer, their body hair was dry. This being a good indication that they were not unduly bothered by the weather, I left them and crawled inch by inch into the tent, peeling off the dripping waterproofs like a lizard shedding its skin.

In the evening I did a stint of 'baby-sitting', while Leonard and Sandra went out to a social evening in Windermere. All the children went to bed without a murmur, but an hour or so later, I discovered little Penny sitting at the foot of the stairs looking very miserable. For a while I could not get a word out of her, then, looking at me with large blue eyes, she cried that she did not want to be 'baby-sat' as she was five years old and not a baby any more. I assured her that the only reason I was in the house was to look after the dog and that I had to come before her parents went out so they could show me where the dog-food was kept.

'Oh, is that why you're here,' she said solemnly, then with a big smile, she hitched up her nightie and padded back upstairs to her room.

The rest of the week was a frustrating mixture of torrential rain and warm sunshine, but at least the medicine seemed to be winning the battle against Thor's bronchial gremlins and the spasms of coughing became less frequent. I managed to explore the valley during the bright spells and when it poured I spent the day browsing through Leonard's marvellous collection of books on local history. In an annexe adjoining the house Leonard's parents had run the local post office since retiring from the family farm. Though well into his eighties, Mr Hayton had the most incredibly sharp memory and a knowledge of the 'innards' of radio and television that was amazing. He enjoyed lively conversation and loved to sit outside his door when the air was warm and put the world to rights for anyone who cared to listen.

'See that big house over yonder?' he said to me one morning, as we sat watching the sun mop up the previous day's rain off the hedgerows. Pointing the stem of his pipe towards a smart house standing in respectable solitude among a mass of flowering shrubs, he continued, 'That used to be the Low Bridge Inn and it was the first pub in England to lose its licence for illegal goings on.'

With a twinkle in his eye, he told me the tale. In the old days in the dales there was not much in the way of entertainment for the local lads, except to gather at the local pub and have a drink or two with their pals on a Saturday night. Trouble was that some of the landlords were not above keeping the ale flowing all night, as long as money was jingling into their pockets. Very few of the isolated spots like Kentmere had their own policeman and a feller from Stavely used to come up on his bike once a week just to have a look around. He always came on the same day each week and, naturally enough, poachers would have taken the day off, late drinkers would have scattered and the door of the Low Bridge Inn would be firmly bolted at closing time. As soon as the man in blue had returned down the valley, licensing hours were swept aside and, with gangs of thirsty navvies building a dam for the new reservoir, the Low Bridge Inn did a roaring trade. It carried on like this for years with the local folk turning a blind eye to the drinking orgies, but when farmers began to find their men too drunk for work and Sunday worshippers were unable to get past heaps of snoring men, sleeping it off in the church porch, complaints flooded in and the landlord ended up in front of the magistrates at Kendal. After a long haranguing match between the opposing parties, the verdict of the Bench was that they 'considered the remoteness from police supervision and the character and necessities of the place and the locality, justified them in refusing to grant the application', and the inn lost its licence.

'Get on with you. Filling the man's head with such rubbish.' Mrs Hayton had been listening to our conversation through the open window. 'You ought to be telling him about what it was like farming hereabouts.' Mr Hayton smiled at his wife's scolding and, striking a match on the wall, sucked the flame into the bowl of his pipe, sending a cloud of smoke drifting across the garden.

'Well,' he continued, as if ignoring the interruption, yet picking up his wife's suggestion, 'life was hard when I was a lad, but with all the new-fangled gadgets they have today, they don't farm any better. There's hardly a feller left that can mend a decent wall gap. Mind you,' he paused to strike another match and apply it to the pipe, 'there were some queer folk about, particularly amongst the landlords. I heard tell of a chap who rented a farm from a well-to-do gent down by Windermere and one day, when he went to pay his rent, the family were at dinner and he was told to sit by the fire until they had finished. The man had travelled a fair distance, as they all did in those days, but no one offered him as much as a cup of tea. "How's the old sow getting on?" asked the landlord, between mouthfuls of pie. "Oh, she's just pigged again," says the farmer, "and one more than she has tits for." "Well, I'm pleased to hear it," said the landlord, "but what does the odd one do when the rest are sucking?" Quick as a flash, the old farmer got in, "It sits and looks on, as I do!"' Mr Hayton was still laughing when I left to give the ponies their medicine.

It poured with rain throughout Saturday and Sunday, but as Thor's cough had gone I decided to leave on Monday, whatever the weather. Admiral Nelson once said that harbours were the ruination of good seamen and the kindness and generosity of the Haytons was such that their house was becoming like the island in Greek mythology, where all who eat the lotus flower forget home and dream their life away. Being British and broke instead of Greek and godly, economic necessity pressurized me to get on with my journey.

CHAPTER 10

Round Trip to Haweswater

Early on Monday morning I opened the tent door to find the cloud lower than ever and torrential rain sluicing down the canvas. It was a dismal scene, with long streamers of water-logged mist draped across the trees like tinsel, while the once proud buttercups lay lifeless in pools of muddy water. A group of chaffinches, who each morning had twittered outside the tent, waiting for my breakfast crumbs, were hunched together for warmth under the shelter of the fly-sheet. I threw them a piece of biscuit, but they ignored it and stared miserably out at the rain. Despite my vow to leave whatever the weather, there did not seem much sense in leaving a comfortable campsite to get soaking wet, so I retreated into the warmth of my sleeping bag and balanced a pan of bubbling porridge on the primus stove. Halfway through my second cup of coffee the patter of rain on the canvas suddenly ceased and I looked out to see the sun bursting through the clouds in a glorious shaft of golden light. The chaffinches came alive and chattered loudly to each other like excited children on a school outing, as the heat drove the mist across the meadows to hang sullenly above the cold waters of the mere. Within an hour the scene was transformed and with a dazzling sun beating down from a clear blue sky I had no excuse to linger for another day. I was busy packing my gear when I heard two of the Hayton girls whispering outside the tent.

'You give them to him,' said one.

'No, you,' said the other, 'you're the oldest.'

Sticking my head out I found little Jaquie Hayton and her sister, Ingrid, holding a tin mug full of buttercups.

'We've brought you these as a going-away present,' said Jaquie, shyly, placing the mug by the tent door.

'It was her idea, she likes you,' burst out Ingrid.

'You rotten thing, what did you have to tell him for,' cried Jaquie and blushing like a beetroot chased Ingrid back to the house. When a chap passes forty and a woman likes him enough to gather him a bunch of flowers, it is a beautiful compliment, even if she is only ten years old.

The ring of the ponies' shoes echoed across the valley as we crossed the stone bridge over the River Kent and turned up a narrow lane by the old inn. In the hedgerows rhododendrons were in full bloom, a sparkling kaleidoscope of colour, washed clean by the rain, filling the air with a gorgeous fragrance as the delicate flowers dried in the warmth of the sun. It was great to be on the move again and I let the ponies find their own pace as the lane climbed steeply above the valley. As we emerged above the trees a magnificent view of upper Kentmere opened out, green meadow land flanking the broad river as it curved towards the natural barrier formed by the undulating ridges of Ill Bell, Froswick and High Street. At a signpost pointing to Nan Bield Pass we turned off into a delightful old drove road carpeted with soft turf and lined with bluebells, red campion and field daisies. As the ponies moved silently over the grass a line of bees droned by, heavily laden with pollen. Groups of lambs, who had been playing 'chase me charlie' round the field stopped to peer curiously over the wall at the strange procession, until a warning snicker sent them scampering back to their mother. Below the collection of farms and cottages at Hollowbank the bridleway disappeared into a morass of bog and we were forced back on to the council's tar and chippings for a short distance, until, at Overend Farm, a stony track followed the edge of an ancient wood to a gate. For some reason the ponies seemed uneasy as we rode through a field beyond the gate and I had to really dig my heels into Thor to get him to move. Jewel just about tugged my arm off as I dragged her along behind me. Rounding a bend in the path I discovered the reason for their reluctance. A huge Highland bull, with horns curving from his head like a pair of sabres, confronted us, pawing the ground as if counting to ten before unleashing his ferocity. By the time he had counted to five we were heading rapidly back to the gate and as the ground shook, announcing he was on his way, I was firmly wiring up the gate. Screeching to a halt, his bloodshot eyes glared at us through the bars as he snorted with frustration and rattled the sabres along the gate. The next time the ponies tried to warn me I would pay attention.

Having clambered amongst a mass of boulders searching for an alternative way round the field, we finally regained the bridlepath and set off towards Smallthwaite Knott where I could see the path zigzagging up to the dip between Harter Fell and Mardale Ill Bell. We were about to cross the ford at Ullstone Gill when I heard the sound of an engine and turned to see a Landrover bounding along the path.

'Where do you think you are going?' said the driver, sourly, as he climbed out of the vehicle.

'I'm making for Mardale,' I replied, 'and since this is a public bridleway what's your objection?'

'Oh, I've no objection, mate,' he continued sneeringly, 'but I've got a stallion ranging about the fell up there and I don't think he'll take very kindly to a pair of strange horses appearing on his patch.' He was certainly right there. A stallion can be far more dangerous than a bull and it would have been asking for trouble to try and take Thor and Jewel past him.

'Look,' I said, 'I've got a long way to go and I can't hang about here all day. Come up with me and get a hold of him so I can get past.'

Climbing into the Landrover, he called, 'Bugger you, mate, my dinner's waiting,' and with a grinding of gears roared away down the track. Cursing the disappearing vehicle I turned the ponies loose while I studied the map to discover we would have to go back past Hollowbank and cross over into Longsleddale and then to Mardale by way of Gatesgarth Pass. It was a long detour and I was in a black mood as the ponies headed back the way we had come.

The hard road was long and tedious and I was thankful to reach the pleasant pack-horse track winding past the old farmhouse of Stile End and across a short moor to Longsleddale. The black mood left me as we jogged steadily along in the shining heat, skylarks singing their hearts out overhead and the musty smell of warm earth all around. It was too nice a day to be wasted fuming about the crazy human race. I relaxed in the saddle and let the music of the jangling harness smooth my ruffled feathers.

The track dipped down by the side of a swift running beck as the deeply gouged valley of Longsleddale came into view far below. Countless rainstorms had swept away the firm surface and I had to lead the ponies carefully down loose shale until the track improved and descended by a wood to cross the River Sprint by an old pack-horse bridge at Sadgill. Since it was Thor's first day out after his illness I did not want to push him too hard, so I rested the ponies and let them graze while I lay back in the shade of a tree. There was not a sign of life anywhere, even in the farms close by the bridge, and I wondered what it must have been like a century or more ago, when teams of pack-horses jangled their way from distant Ravenglass, through Eskdale, Ambleside and Troutbeck, over the track we had just crossed from Kentmere. One of the farms would very probably have been an inn for it was an important point, where cattle drovers and pack-horse drivers crossed the river with their animals. At one time there was only a ford, but although the river is not very wide, it was so often in spate due to the heavy rainfall of the area, it was impossible to cross it for several days at a time. In the early eighteenth century the inhabitants of the townships along the great highway petitioned for a bridge to be built because, 'a water or rivulet called Sadgill is often raised and overflows its banks so that no passenger dare venture to cross the same and many times travellers are forced to stay two or three days before they dare venture to cross and are often in danger of their cattle being lost in the crossing'. The petition was favourably received and a bridge was built.

I gave Thor his medicine and we set off along an easy track towards the head of the valley. On either side the fell rose steeply from the valley floor, forming a gigantic gorge with the rocky precipices of Goat Scar and Buckbarrow Crag frowning at each other across the valley. Climbing round the foot of Buckbarrow, the track deteriorated into a mass of loose scree and progress was painfully slow as the ponies struggled to get a grip. Higher up, the owners of Wrengill Quarry had strengthened the surface with a 'staircase' of slate slabs laid on edge. Although this surface was not easy for a pony to walk on, it was a lot less laborious than the scree and we crept steadily upwards by a broad beck that foamed and tumbled in a series of waterfalls below the track. Above the waterfalls the track levelled out and curved round to a sheep fold where the wide track ended and numerous stone cairns followed an erratic course up the soggy fellside ahead, indicating the line of Gatesgarth Pass. A molten sun beat down unmercifully as we slipped and skidded up the washed-out path in a welter of mud and sweat and it was a blessed relief to reach the summit of the pass above Mardale. The heat was intense and Thor and Jewel slurped what they could from a minute trickle of water among the rocks while I drained the juice from an orange like a vacuum pump. My shirt was saturated with sweat so I peeled it off and hung it on a fence post, letting the hot sun evaporate the rivulets running down my back. Within ten minutes the shirt was bone dry and, heaving the ever-searching muzzles out of the rough grass, we continued on down the old pack-horse track to the edge of Haweswater and the surfaced road.

Expecting to find a quiet, rarely visited valley, I was amazed to see a mass of cars parked where the road terminated and people swarmed like ants over the grass, having picnics or hurling stones into the beck. Tying the ponies to a rickety signpost I sat on a rock, scanning the area for a peaceful spot to pitch the tent. Below me a mother and brood were perched nervously on a large boulder while Dad squinted through the family box camera, bawling instructions like Sam Goldwyn directing a film epic.

'Mother, I can't take it while you're hanging on with both hands, it's not Everest you know. Sandra, pull your skirt over your knees, you look positively indecent. Tony and Michael, if you two don't stop arguing you'll go back to the car.'

I retreated from the bedlam and leaving the ponies, walked on a little way up the path leading to Small Water. To my delight I found a large stone sheep-pen with a good fence round it. There was no water and more stones than grass, but it was ideal to put the ponies in for the night. Returning to collect the ponies, I found Jewel trussed up like a chicken with the lead rope around her legs. She had been busy mowing the grass round and round the post and with every turn the rope got shorter until it finally held her so tight she could not move. It took half and hour of pushing and heaving before I managed to get her free and with the pair of them safely in the sheep-pen I flopped wearily onto the grass. It was late afternoon and the last of the picnickers were trooping down to their cars to be home in time for their tea. Mud-caked children, soaking dogs, empty Thermos flasks, fishing nets, sheep skulls, an assortment of wild flowers and Grandma were all packed into the family Mini. Finally the last car departed in the wake of a long convoy and peace descended over the valley. Sheep drifted down to forage among the discarded sandwiches and orange peel and a few crows hopped about squabbling over bits of chocolate paper.

The level of Haweswater was very low and the stone walls marking the fields of the one-time hamlet of Mardale had appeared, bare and lifeless, like an exhumed skeleton. In the 1920s, for the benefit of the thirsty Mancunians, the Corporation of Manchester built a dam across the end of Haweswater, raising the level by some ninety-five feet and drowning a school, the Dun Bull Inn, four farms and a church. Far from the main tourist honey-pots, Mardale was an isolated backwater, little frequented by visitors and months would pass without a stranger being seen. There is a story about a guest staying at the Dun Bull, during the month of June, complaining that the beer was off.

'Why that's queer,' said the landlord, 'it was fresh enough at grouse time.' (The previous August.)

The Dun Bull carried on the tradition of centuries as a great meeting-place for shepherds and huntsmen and today any attempt at desecrating such a part of Lakeland heritage would be met with impassioned speeches and protest marches. Unfortunately for Mardale, in the 1920s cash had more influence than conservation.

As the sun sank towards the flat ridge of High Street a lively breeze bounced off the crags, stirring up the dust in the sheep-pen and whipping the flat surface of Haweswater into white caps. The temperature plummeted and there was a chilly nip in the air as I checked the ponies and left them with a canvas bucket full of water. Hurriedly pitching the tent I was thankful to crawl inside. The primus soon heated a pan of soup and by the time I had finished eating the wind was tearing down the valley and cracking the canvas like a bullwhip. It sounded as if it was heralding another session of bad weather and sure enough, when I looked out a seething mass of black cloud obscured the fell tops and was rapidly eating up the blue sky. With the darkness came rain and the wind increased to gale force, battering the tent with such vicious gusts several guy lines were flogged to shreds. The abrupt change in the weather affected poor old Thor and his cough started again. All night the gale screamed and howled, lashing the tent with torrential rain and all night Thor's racking cough broke through the din as the bitterly cold wind had him gasping for breath. It was impossible to sleep and the hours ticked agonizingly by as I tossed and turned, waiting for the dawn. At last a few shreds of grey light crept across the valley and I crawled out to see what I could do for Thor. The view from the tent was depressing. Although the wind had almost dropped, thick cloud hung low over Haweswater and a cold, clammy drizzle drifted across the saturated landscape. Becks that yesterday trickled quietly amongst warm rocks were now roaring torrents, bursting with peaty water, pouring from the high fells and crags. Silvery moisture hung about the carpet of thick heather all around the tent and dripped monotonously from the wire fence of the sheep-pen. The ponies stood miserably behind the gate of the pen, trying to get what protection they could and Thor's cough seemed to rattle every rib as his large frame shook with each wheezy spasm. Looking at my two faithful friends, rain running down their faces and the breeze stirring the lank hair of their manes, I realized we could not continue the journey and we must turn for home. It was terribly disappointing, but the welfare of that dear old pony was more important. The pack-horse routes I would miss had been in existence for many hundreds of years, they would still be there another day.

Whatever Thor's complaint was, fortunately it did not appear to be contagious. Jewel had never uttered as much as a sneeze since we set off and was bursting with health. The rain increased as I slowly packed and loaded the sodden heap on to her back. A quick check to see nothing had been left behind and away we went, kicking up clouds of spray as the ponies' feet drove through the wet heather.

It would have been quicker to go over the Nan Bield Pass instead of back over Gatesgarth, but not wanting to meet the stallion, I played safe and we tramped up the winding route we had descended so eagerly the previous day. To ease the strain on his breathing I walked beside Thor, but, cough or no cough, he stormed up the path and trying to keep up with him I was worn out by the time we reached the top. The rain stopped, but in the cloud, visibility was reduced to a few feet and we floundered through bog and stumbled over the cairns marking the route. By the abandoned workings of Wrengill Quarry the mist lifted and below the sprawling valley of Longsleddale glistened as the sun reflected off the wet meadows. The day brightened considerably as we reached Sadgill and with the damp atmosphere behind us, Thor's cough eased to a splutter. Following the drove road we crossed to Kentmere and by mid-afternoon the ponies were once more chewing the grass in Leonard Hayton's field.

CHAPTER 11

Hagg End Farm

The next morning I woke to find the sun beaming down from a cloudless sky. With such violent extremes of weather as I had been experiencing, it is hardly surprising that the subject is the number one topic of conversation in Britain and foreigners often accuse us of having nothing else to talk about. Our unpredictable climate is exciting at times, but I was beginning to wish it would make its mind up.

I hoped to reach Hagg End, near Stavely, that day, where two good friends, Geoff and Margaret Ibbotson, farmed and I was hurrying with my packing when an attractive girl looked over the wall, admiring the ponies. The subject of horses opened the conversation and the packing was forgotten while we talked about bridleways and a pony she owned. In the course of the conversation she told me her name was Selina Tutin and although a qualified botanist, she was working as a housekeeper at Brathay Field Centre near Ambleside. Having been an instructor at Brathay myself, some years ago, I was interested to hear what changes had taken place. Two hours passed before she managed to escape and continue her walk. I told Selina I would call at Brathay when I left Hagg End and she arranged to meet me on her pony at the Windermere ferry.

The sun was high in the sky when I waved good-bye to the Haytons and rode up the hill past the church to join the bridleway leading to Kentmere Hall. Despite the bright morning, the sky to the west looked gloomy and long streaks of cirrus cloud warned of another unsettled spell. In the yard of the hall, now a farm, I tied the ponies to a post while I took some photgraphs of the ancient pele tower. Originally built as a protection from the Scots raiders, the hall was later built against it and made the name of Hugh Hird, the Troutbeck giant, famous throughout history. During the building of the hall he is said to have lifted a beam into position over the kitchen fire-place, that had defeated the efforts of ten men to move it. He was a favourite of the lord of the manor, who once sent him to London with a message for the king. When he was asked what he would like for his dinner, he replied 'the sunny side of a wether'. The servants, discovering that a wether was a sheep, but not knowing which side he wanted, served the whole animal and ravenous Hugh ate the lot. If he was alive today he would be much sought after to advertise a well-known Irish brew, made from the waters of the Liffey.

It started to rain as I led the ponies away from the hall and climbed the steep path to Whiteside End. The view over Kentmere was magnificent for a while, but as the rain increased the clouds rolled down off the fell and blotted out everything within a radius of two hundred yards. The firm path gradually deteriorated and at Park Beck disappeared into a morass of waterlogged moss. Leaving the ponies fastened to a gate, I went ahead to reconnoitre the route and was stopped in my tracks by the sound of someone crying. Moving cautiously through the mist I discovered a young couple clinging together for warmth and the girl sobbing her heart out. Between chattering teeth the lad explained they had left their car by Kentmere Church and had got lost when the mist came down. They were both so cold they could hardly speak, so I gave them a tot of rum each and walked back with them until they were safely on the broad path leading to Kentmere Hall.

Trudging back through the rain I rejoined the ponies and carried on the search for a way round the bog. With the help of the compass I found a thin path leading to a gate in the wall and beyond a broad lane descended gently through innumerable gates to a surfaced road and the little hamlet of

Grassgarth. The rain eased off and the sun broke through the murk, but it did not like what it saw and disappeared almost immediately, leaving an ominous wad of black cloud that promised to empty a chamber-pot on us at any moment.

Reaching the main Kendal to Windermere road at Ings, a torrent of vehicles poured past in both directions and we waited an hour before I managed to persuade a kind motorist to stop and let us cross over. Waving my thanks I pulled the ponies after me and raced across into the sanctuary of the narrow road leading to Hagg End Farm.

Geoff and Margaret were busy shearing sheep when we arrived in the farmyard and the scent of wool and marking fluid drifted across from the pens. They were rushing to get done before the threatening clouds opened the sluice gates and, pausing only to give me a quick wave, Margaret grabbed a sheep and dragged it, struggling, to where Geoff's shears removed its woolly overcoat in half a dozen deft strokes. A dab of red marking fluid on its flank and it was released into another pen, all head and legs, looking very self-conscious in its newly-shorn nakedness. The rain arrived with a vengeance as the last fleece was being pushed into the large wool-sack and there was a mad scramble to get it into the barn before it got soaked. Heaving the packs and saddles under a farm trailer I turned the ponies loose and ran for the shelter of the house as the deluge reached monsoon proportions and turned the earth yard into a quagmire.

It was warm and cosy in the stone-flagged kitchen. Flames danced in the big open fire, glinting on polished horse brasses nailed along the massive beams and illuminating faded sepia photographs hung about the room, showing shepherds working with sheep and horses proudly displaying rosettes at long forgotten agricultural shows. Margaret lifted a smoke-blackened kettle off the hob and we sat round the scrubbed-topped table devouring thick slices of ham and fresh bread, washed down with strong brown tea.

Mr Walker, who lived with the Ibbotsons and had farmed at Hagg End most of his eighty-three years, was keen to hear about the ponies and the way I carried the load on the pack-saddle. He had worked with horses all his life and had a fund of tales about the tricks unscrupulous dealers got up to to disguise lameness or bad character. On one occasion he bought a Clydesdale from a man, who assured him it was broken to the plough, but each time he hitched it up the animal bolted across the field and jumped the fence, dragging the plough with it.

'Maybe I heard him wrong,' said Mr Walker, with a wry smile, 'perhaps it had broken a plough.'

There was once a horse working in the woods around Windermere that was so intelligent that all the men had to do was hitch the drag-chain to a felled tree and the horse would haul it down to the road and under a block and tackle hung on a gantry, so efficiently that they could lift the log straight on to a waggon. He would then return up the hill on his own and repeat the process without any supervision. If a log jammed against a rock as it was being hauled down, the horse would stand and whinny until someone came to free it.

Mr Walker remembered the farms at Mardale selling up, prior to being submerged under Haweswater. As was the custom in those days, farmers gathered from miles around to attend the sale and give the outgoing tenant a good 'send-off'. It was a terrible day, with rain and gales, and half-way up Shap Fell, on the old A6, the bus carrying a contingent of farmers from the Windermere district overheated and ground to a halt. Eager not to miss the sale, the passengers piled out and pushed the bus to the top of the fell before gaily free-wheeling down the other side. After the sale the old bus bulged with scythes, rakes, spades, butter-churns, harness, drums of sheep dip, shears and a vast assortment of bits and pieces dear to the heart of a farmer.

Through the kitchen window I could see that the rain had almost stopped so, retrieving the pack from under the trailer, I squelched through the wet grass and pitched the tent by the side of the house. The last peg of the fly-sheet was being knocked in when the heavens opened again and throwing the bags into the tent I dived in after them. There was not a breath of wind and the rain dropped from the inky sky vertically, as if I had camped under a waterfall. I had been invited to spend the evening with the Ibbotsons, but it poured so hard I would have been soaked even crossing the short distance to the house. Lighting the primus, I warmed the inside of the tent and got down to darning huge holes in my socks and repairing numerous tears in my anorak.

Throughout the night my sleep was constantly disturbed by the pounding of the rain on the tent and at first light I got up, stiff and bleary-eyed, to make a mug of coffee. Outside it was a wet dreary world. Water cascaded off the barn roof and surged through the yard in a river of black mud, cow dung and bits of straw. On through the gate it swept, lapping under the wheels of a silent tractor, vivid colours streaking the dark surface as diesel fuel dripped onto it from a loose pipe. Down the track by the tent it gurgled, sweeping all before it, spinning in a maelstrom of flotsam as it disappeared down an overburdened culvert.

The clank of buckets from the byre signalled it was milking time and I went across to see if I could help. While Margaret milked that two Ayrshires I fed the calves and held onto the rubber-teated bottles as orphan lambs slurped warm milk from their artificial mothers. In the kitchen the new milk was sieved and left to cool while breakfast was prepared. Rashers of home-cured bacon sizzled in a large pan alongside the rich yellow yolks of fresh laid eggs. Toast was made by the simple method of holding a piece of bread in front of the fire on the end of a wire toasting fork. There was no electricity in the farmhouse, yet breakfast took no more time and effort to prepare without the electrical gadgets considered essential in the majority of homes today.

Geoff left for a cattle sale immediately after breakfast and Margaret, having got the children off to school, prepared to go to Kendal to collect a pig from the abattoir. The ponies seemed happy enough with a large field of grass to chew at and with no sign of the rain letting up there was little point in moving on, so I climbed into the Landrover and went to Kendal with Margaret.

Despite the weather, the town thronged with people dashing in and out of the shops, jostling with each other along the pavements as they rushed to escape from the downpour. I retreated into the library to see if I could find any new information about the pack-horse routes. In its day Kendal had been one of the main centres of commerce in the north of England, particularly for the wool trade, and I felt sure that somewhere in the library's vast local collection there would be references to the pack-horse trade. I discovered a book by a very brave and determined lady called Celia Fiennes, who, in the eighteenth century, explored England on horseback, and riding side-saddle at that. She was not very impressed with the roads of the Lake District and commented, 'There can be no carriages, but only very narrow ones, like wheelbarrows, that with a horse they convey fuel and all things else. They also use a horse on which they have a sort of pannyers, some closed, some open, that they strew full of hay, turf, lime or dung and everything they would use and the reason is plain from the narrowness of the roads.' A history of Kendal provided me with some marvellous gems about the pack-horse traffic and I was amazed to read that at one time over three hundred gangs of pack-horses plied regularly between Kendal and the major market towns of the country. The report listed the movement of pack-horses as one gang of twenty to and from London every week; one gang of eighteen to Wigan weekly; one gang of twenty to Whitehaven via Wrynose and Hardknott; one gang of fifteen to Cockermouth; two gangs of twenty-six to Barnard Castle; two gangs of fifteen twice a week to Penrith; one gang of fifteen twice a week to Settle; one gang of ten to York weekly; one gang of five to Ulveston and one of six to Hawkshead twice weekly; one gang of six to Appleby twice a week; one gang of six to Cartmel; and a gang of twenty-four every six weeks to Glasgow. It must have been a grand sight as they wound through the narrow streets of the town loaded with all manner of merchandise and led by a smart bell horse.

Leaving the quiet of the library, I went out into the rain and walked to the pub where I had arranged to meet Margaret. It was crowded with lunchtime drinkers, but we managed to find seats at a table and ordered pork pie and pickles. The opposite side of our table was occupied by two smartly turned out gents, who from their conversation, were obviously local government officials. Blue suit was complaining to grey suit that X should not have been put up for chairman of such and such a committee for he had not anything like the experience he had. Prodding grey suit with his knife he continued, 'I am sure you would agree, old chap, that were it not for me the whole department would have gone to pieces long ago.' Grey suit, by this time, had a mouthful of chips and could not speak, but nodded his head vigorously with approval. The conversation subsided for a minute or two and I had a forkful of pie on its way to my mouth when blue suit blurted out, 'I have been wondering how I can get sewage back from the water authority.' Returning the pie to the plate I listened while he outlined his strategy for ascending to glory as head of sewage disposal. Suddenly the mountains, green fields and the clear air seemed far away and I longed to be amongst them, listening to farmers and country folk talking hard-headed sense on matters of value and importance. Leaving my meal half eaten I steered Margaret out into the rain.

Collecting the carcass of the pig from the abattoir, we returned to the farm and spent the evening cutting it into joints. Before going to the tent for the night I splashed across to check the ponies and give Thor a hefty dose of cough mixture. Although it had poured down continually since we arrived, they both seemed unconcerned by the soaking. The rain was still hammering on the tent when I fell asleep.

I slept well and was raring to go the next morning, but still the rain poured unceasingly down. After breakfast I phoned home to discover that Border Television had been trying to find me to film an interview and would I contact them. I eventually got through to a producer and arranged to let him know when I reached Brathay Hall.

Margaret loaded the Landrover with the joints of pork to take down to her mother's deep freeze in Stavely and I went along for the ride. Over coffee Mrs Holmes told me some fascinating stories about the days when her parents farmed close to Hilltop, Beatrix Potter's home at Sawrey, on the west side of Lake Windermere. As a young girl Mrs Holmes often went with her father to have the farm horses shod at the local smithy and Beatrix Potter, or Mrs Heelis as she then was, would be sitting by the forge, listening to the village gossip. Although very gifted, she had a reputation for being rather crusty. One day, after a severe rainstorm, Mrs Holmes's father went to rescue some of his cattle stranded in a rapidly rising pool of water, caused by a blocked drain. To release the flow he kicked a hole in the wall and the water poured across the adjacent field. Within minutes a familiar figure in wide-brimmed hat, came striding across the meadows.

'Kirkbride, who gave you authority to release that water

over my property?' she demanded.

A canny Scotsman, he leaned on his stick and replied drily, 'Mrs Heelis, when you discover how to turn water uphill I won't send it down your fields,' and leaving her speechless went back to his cows. Maybe Beatrix Potter was equally canny and replied in a more subtle way by portraying Mr Kirkbride as Tommy Brock, the badger, in the *Tale of Mr Tod*.

In the evening the rain stopped and the incredibly beautiful sunset set the fells ablaze with the colour of molten gold. Sheep emerged from under hedgerows, shaking water off their backs and the trees came alive with the sounds of twittering birds. On a rock above the farmhouse a big dog fox casually surveyed the countryside, then, jumping down, loped effortlessly across the fellside, clearing a wall and ditch in one mighty leap. As darkness settled steadily over the quiet fells, sheep, ponies, trees and rocks all merged together and faded into the velvet night.

Under the dark beams of the kitchen, the soft glow of the oil lamp cast shadows across the collection of china dogs, jugs of flowers and family photographs scattered about the Welsh dresser. A tall grandfather clock ticked loudly from the half light of an alcove, growling with anticipation as the hands reached the half hour, its aged mechanism never quite managing a chime. By the polished range old Mr Walker dozed in his favourite rocking chair, a fat tabby cat curled in a fluffy ball on his lap. Margaret brought out a battered shoe box full of faded photographs of the Lake District and we sat round the table sorting through them. Grim-faced men in stove-pipe hats and ladies in voluminous dresses stared stonily from formal wedding poses of nearly a century ago. A picture of an RSPCA sign at the foot of Kirkstone Pass entreated all coach passengers to walk up the steep sections for the sake of the horses. There were numerous photographs of bewhiskered gentlemen shearing sheep or sitting on carts loaded with hay. I unearthed a rather odd postcard showing a large waggon with solid tyres, lying on its side, with the caption 'Thirlmere Accident'. Apparently, in the early 1900s a travelling circus was passing Wythburn Church, by the side of Thirlmere, when the steam traction-engine towing a trailer carrying cages of animals went out of control and plunged through the wall and down the embankment into the lake. It was a complete wreck and lay there for many years as a bizarre tourist attraction and an enterprising local photographer did a roaring trade selling postcards of the scene.

The late weather forecast on the radio promised the return of warm weather and when I went out to the tent millions of stars blazed from a clear sky, picking out patches of soft white mist drifting around the fields.

CHAPTER 12

Brathay

The weather man was right. It was the most perfect morning and I lost no time in packing the gear and saddling up the ponies. Waving goodbye to the Ibbotsons and Mr Walker I guided Thor down a narrow lane and onto the main road leading to Bowness and the ferry. The sun had brought the motorists out and they stormed by, hooting loudly, making the ponies so jumpy I put Jewel on a short lead rope and led Thor along a thin strip of grass at the side of the road.

Peggy Crossland, the Secretary of the Fell Pony Society, had invited me to call at her home on the outskirts of Bowness, but though we passed several houses none fitted the description. I was beginning to think I had missed it when I saw a Fell pony in a field close by a large rambling house.

Miss Crossland gave us a warm welcome and, with Thor and Jewel tied securely to a gate, well away from her rose bushes, she invited me into the house for a cup of tea. In the comfortable lounge of the Crossland's beautiful old house, I worked my way through a plateful of home-made scones and cake while she talked enthusiastically about the Fell ponies she had owned. She had an incredible memory for names and could reel off sires and dams going back almost to the day when the pony was first recognized as a native breed.

'How far back in history does the Fell pony go?' I asked, between mouthfuls of delicious sponge cake.

'Well, we've no actual proof,' she replied, 'but we think very probably they were known to the Romans. Someone sent me a reference to that recently. Let me see if I can find it.' Turning to a lovely ornate desk, she rummaged through a stack of papers. 'Yes, here it is. It's from Bulmer's *History of*

Cumberland. I won't read it all, but there are some interesting bits in it.' Turning to the window to get more light, she read, 'When Caesar enquired the origin of those inhabiting the Northern part of the country he was informed that they were divided into tribes, the most important being the Brigantes who inhabited the counties of Yorkshire, Durham, Cumberland, Westmorland and Lancashire. They were as wild as the hills in which they dwelt. They live in hovels in the ground and fight in chariots, having small, fleet horses.' Placing the paper back on the desk Miss Crossland went on, 'That is probably the first reference to the Fell pony in history and if so they have been around a long time. Of course, that's only speculation, but what we are sure of is that the Fell pony that we know today originated in Galloway in Southern Scotland and, in fact, there are still a lot of old folk who refer to them as Fell Galloways. In those days they would roam in wild herds, but as agriculture became more intensified they would be forced out into the rough ground and eventually into the mountainous country of the Lake District. The father of the breed was a stallion found roaming around Stainmore, saddled and bridled, after Prince Charlie's army retreated north in 1746. They found him cropping ling and gave him the name "Lingcropper".'

'How would you describe the perfect Fell pony?' I asked.

'Well, you've got to know the type to appreciate the points of a good Fell pony and that's probably why they don't do so well in the "Mountain and Moorland" classes at shows. Often the judges are not sure what they are looking for. What we like to see in a good Fell pony is a deep body, strong, with plenty of bone, and long mane and tail, short back with good weight-carrying ability. It must have a pony head with big nostrils, a fine muzzle, big eyes and a broad forehead. They must also look as if they are capable of living out all the year round. And another thing,' she continued, remembering an important point, 'when they are moving they should pick up their feet and use their knees and hocks, but not exaggeratedly like a Hackney or they would batter their feet to bits on rocky ground.'

'What about height?' I said.

'There is no minimum height, although I would consider a pony under twelve hands high to be too small. The best height is thirteen point one hands high to thirteen point three hands high and anything over fourteen hands high we don't like at all.'

'Most Fell ponies I have seen are black in colour. Is this essential?' I enquired.

'Oh goodness me, no! It is the type that is more important. Fell ponies can be either black, brown or grey. Some people are under the impression that a black pony must not have any white on it, but this is not true. A white star can be attractive and a little white on a leg, around the coronet, is not objected to. Too much white usually means there is cross breeding somewhere back, probably Dales, which have some Clydesdale influence.'

'From what I've read,' I said, 'the Fell pony was used a great deal as a pack-horse throughout the Lake District, but what other uses did it have?'

'Well it was certainly the farmer's friend and I doubt if any dales farm could have existed without having a few of them. You see, there were a lot more farms in the old days than there are now and most of them had very steep land. They used to yoke four ponies to a wooden plough and cultivate the land in long strips called rig and furrow. You can still see the strips today on any steep pasture. They pulled wooden sledges at haytime because you wouldn't dare take a trailer on some of those steep fields. In many places they were used for shepherding and, in fact, they are still used a lot for this work on the hills of Lanarkshire and other places in Southern Scotland.'

'I believe Fell ponies were renowned for their speed when

trotting,' I said.

'Ah yes,' replied Miss Crossland, looking wistfully at a photograph hung on the wall. 'I remember a time when we had one of our Fell mares in harness and my sister got very cross with me because she had to gallop her pony to keep up on the way to Windermere. Mind you, they weren't bred to trot, it was something that just evolved out of friendly competition between the farmers. Every farmer would have a trap to go to market in and, of course, when they met together there would be an awful lot of boasting about who had the best pony and who could get home the fastest. A pony was never allowed to canter when pulling a trap and, over the years, the long stride developed and a good Fell pony can trot as fast as some horses can canter.'

'Looking at a map of the Lake District, it is noticeable that many of the bridleways lead up to quarries. Were Fell ponies used by the quarrymen?' I asked.

'Oh yes. Carrying slates in panniers on the sides of ponies was the only way it could be got down in the early days, particularly from quarries like the ones high up on Honister Pass and Coniston Old Man. I'm not sure if they were used in the mines in the Lake District, but they were certainly a favourite in the mines of Northumberland. The miners were very fond of them on account of their willingness and intelligence. Two-year-old colts were gathered in off the fells and sold at Brough Hill Fair in the autumn. They were let to run on rough ground around the mines until they were four years old, then broken in for hauling tubs in the mines. The miners shaved their tails so as not to collect too much dust.'

Outside in the garden I could hear Thor and Jewel stamping impatiently and, looking at the clock, I was amazed to find it was almost midday. Pulling on her coat, Miss Crossland insisted on coming to the ferry and helping me across with the ponies. As I was tightening girths and checking the pack I asked her what she thought the future was for the Fell pony and the society.

'The breed's going from strength to strength,' she said proudly, 'and membership has topped six hundred and is gaining every year. More and more people are beginning to appreciate the attraction of these strong and willing little ponies and a number have recently been exported to the continent and Scandinavia. I have bred them for over thirty years and as far as I am concerned there is nothing to beat them.'

There was a long queue of cars waiting at the landing, but I walked to the head and asked the driver of the leading car if I could nip on in front of him. He was extremely pleasant and his family crowded round, feeding the ponies with sweets and bombarding me with questions about my journey. Thor snorted apprehensively as the ferry clanked to a halt in front of him, but Jewel trotted happily up the ramp accompanied by Miss Crossland. The ferryman squeezed as many cars on board as he could and we were pressed uncomfortably into a corner next to a shiny saloon car. Every time Jewel shifted a leg the pack swung close to the smart paintwork and the driver paled with fright. Unable to stand it any longer he wound his window down.

'Hey, mate,' he pleaded, 'it's taken me years to save up for this car and I've only had it a week. Do me a favour and keep that damned brute away from it will you.'

Jewel looked a bit upset at being called a 'damned brute', but I did my best to oblige, by wedging myself between the pack and his sacred enamel. The ferry chugged across the mirror-like surface of Windermere and within minutes the ramp grounded on the concrete apron below the Freshwater Biological Laboratory at Ferry House. Miss Crossland had been a great help with the ponies on the crowded ferry and I was most grateful. With a cheery wave she departed for home, to prepare for a Fell pony show. An absolute ball of energy, it is mainly due to her enthusiasm and dedication that the Fell Pony Society has continued to flourish and attract more members over the years.

A line of cars edged impatiently past as we made our way along the narrow road behind Ferry House, but they need not have bothered, we soon turned into a narrow lane below Claife Heights, thankful to leave the road behind. After a mile or so the metal surface ended at the edge of a wood and a good track continued on beneath an arch of tall trees. Shut off from the sun, it was dark and creepy in the wood and the hair at the back of my neck tingled as I thought of the story of the crier of Claife. During a dark and stormy night in the fifteenth century, a call for the ferry boat was heard, coming from the Sawrey side of the lake. Although it was blowing a gale the boatman rowed across, but when he returned he was as white as a sheet and struck dumb with terror. Within a few days he died and for a long time afterwards, whenever the night was stormy, screams and yells were heard in the wood above the ferry landing and no boatman dared cross. It is said that even when the foxhounds are in full cry through the wood they suddenly stop and refuse to go any further. I am not a person who readily accepts ghost stories, but I do not believe in tempting providence either and I felt a lot easier when the trees thinned out and the sun returned.

In the mud along the track I noticed a line of hoofprints and I wondered if Selina had come to meet me. Because of the uncertainty of the weather I had not bothered to let her know I was on my way. The track followed the edge of the lake beneath giant spruce, larch and rhododendrons. All the way the views were superb. Graceful yachts sailed majestically by, sharp bows cleaving a silvery passage through the blue water as a zephyr of wind pressed against the sails. Across the lake the tree-lined meadows of the farmland rose from the water's edge, bright emerald green against a dark back-cloth of high fells towering above Troutbeck and Ambleside. It was so breathtaking I let the ponies graze and sat spellbound for an hour on a rocky knoll above Bell Grange House.

Beyond Bell Grange a surfaced road led to the tiny hamlet of High Wray and on past Wray Castle to the main Hawkshead to Ambleside road. I could hear the whine of traffic long before the road came into sight and trying to ride along it was a nightmare. Coaches, cars and motorbikes blocked the highway in an endless procession, never conceding an inch to each other, let alone a fool trying to keep two ponies from jumping over the hedge. We were swept along by this loathsome tide until I was able to dash the ponies into a lane leading to Pull Wyke Bay on the edge of the Brathay Estate. A quiet ride along a woodland path brought us to the hall, then on to the field centre. Several determined thumps on the front door brought no response and I was about to return to the ponies when Selina appeared from a nearby cottage. I was not actually welcomed with opened arms and wondered why the reception was a bit icy, when I remembered the hoofprints by the ferry. Then it all came out. She had been to meet me all right, not in today's gorgeous sunshine, but in yesterday's torrential rain. Having shivered at the ferry for a couple of hours she had set off back, soaked and swearing. I could only apologize and promise to take her to a pub later that evening for a peace-making pint.

I found a moss patch for the tent on a wooded headland with a lovely view over the lake and then Selina led the way to a field where she grazed her pony. He was a handsome cob of about fourteen hands high and after an introductory bout of kicking and squealing settled down with Thor and Jewel like an old friend.

It was a fantastic evening as I sat outside the tent eating my dinner and I was so engrossed in watching a pair of mallard dodging in and out of the reeds with their brood of youngsters, I almost forgot about meeting Selina. I compared my two shirts to see which was the least dirty, scrubbed patches of mud off my jeans and with hair neatly held in place with a cupful of Lake Windermere, presented myself at Selina's cottage, the perfect beau. She did not say much, but for some reason kept her car window open all the way to the pub.

When I crawled into my sleeping-bag later that night I had drunk rather more than my customary measure and some idiot was aggravating the situation by rocking the headland from side to side.

The sound of church bells roused me next morning and looking at my watch I was staggered to find it was eleven o'clock. My mouth felt as if I had been chewing cinders and inside my head a little gnome was trying to chop his way out with an axe. Flinging open the tent door, I ran naked down to the lake and jumped in. The initial shock of the icy water took my breath away, but I soon warmed up and swam around the little bay before climbing out to get dressed. I felt tremendous. The headache had gone, leaving behind a ravenous appetite and I made a large dent in my bacon ration as slice after slice was flung into the pan. Listening to the bells echoing across the valley as I leant against a tree with a cup of coffee, I realized it must be Sunday and there was no point in phoning Border Television. It meant having to stay another day, but that did not matter. The weather was really making up for lost time and as the weather improved so did Thor's cough. I was a bit short of cash but I would just have to eat less. For the moment the world was a wonderful place and when Selina came down and said she had got the afternoon off and did I fancy riding over Loughrigg Fell I jumped at the chance.

Poor Jewel made a terrible racket when we left her behind and stormed up and down the field in a rage.

Leaving Brathay we walked the ponies slowly along a

quiet back road by Brathay Church. It was one of those superb days we often get in early summer in the Lake District when, after a cold night, with a hint of frost, the air is crystal clear with a bright sun filtering through the greens and yellows of the oaks and sycamores, highlighting the soft pastel shades of the wild flowers in the hedgerows. Rising gently, the road wound up to Spy Hill by the hamlet of Skelwith Fold, then dropped again to Skelwith, where an old pack-horse bridge spans the River Brathay. At one time the bridge was noted for magical cures for various ailments and according to local belief, a person suffering from whooping cough could be cured by riding over the bridge on a donkey, facing the animal's tail. As we rode across I let Thor sniff at the stonework, hoping that the magic might have more effect on his ailing bronchial system that modern antibiotics. It seems that fairy cures lose their potency with age, much the same as our chemical concoctions. Thor coughed heavily as we sweated up the steep track by the side of Neaum Wood. At Tarn Foot cottages the angle eased off and we let the ponies graze for a few minutes while Selina and I sheltered under the trees. The clear air had given way to a thick purple haze and it was incredibly hot. Visions of the previous night's cool lager and lime floated tantalizingly by as I searched among the rocks for water, but there was not as much as a drop in the dried-up dust beds that in rainy weather were lusty becks.

Leaving Tarn Foot the stony path gave way to firm turf and skirting round the foot of Ivy Crag, climbed easily up the lower slopes of Loughrigg to a grassy plateau and a fine view of the twin spurs of Rydal and Scondale Fell, rising from the valley to merge together on the summit of Fairfield. Selina tore away to exercise her great cob, but I kept Thor to a steady walk and met up with her again by the long abandoned Ambleside golf course. From the old club house a surfaced road snaked steeply down the fellside and the ponies had great difficulty keeping their feet on the smooth asphalt. Reaching the River Rothay we joined an old road that had been an important highway for pack-horses, and later the mail coaches with their sturdy teams of horses. From Rydal its winding course was dictated by the meanderings of the river, but progress demanded a more direct route to Ambleside and a new road was carved through the meadow land of Rydal Park.

There were quite a lot of cars about, but nothing like the solid crocodile that confronted us when we reached the outskirts of Ambleside at Rothay Bridge. The weekenders and daytrippers were flooding out of the dales to join the long queue creeping bumper to bumper through Ambleside, along the edge of Lake Windermere and through the bottleneck of Stavely to explode in a competition of superior engine power on the M6, at Kendal. Mini buses crowded with climbers, majestic Jaguars and Rovers, family saloons full of sleepy children, sports cars with hoods down to show off gorgeous blonde passengers, all having come to pay homage to the great open air, were now making their exodus to the bed-sitters, council estates and comfortable suburbia of Leeds, Manchester, Birmingham and beyond. The air was thick with acrid exhaust fumes and the smell of hot rubber, as the endless convoy moved slowly forward and, although it was obvious we wanted to cross the road, we were completely ignored until a sweet smile from Selina had a delighted old gentleman standing on his brakes to let us pass. Keeping to the grass verge, we dashed through Clappersgate and escaped into the peace of the Brathay Estate.

Later that evening Selina's little car whisked us up to the Drunken Duck, a cheerful pub perched on a hill midway between Ambleside and Hawkshead. In the halcyon days when I was an instructor at Brathay Hall, it was a favourite gathering place of the staff and many an end of course report was written in the lounge, after closing time, amid great hilarity and breaks for fierce darts tournaments. The pub has changed hands since those days, but the present owners have retained the traditional atmosphere, resisting the fashion common to many Lakeland hostelries of filling up good drinking space with a caterwauling juke box and adding another nail to the coffin of conversation.

Standing at the junction of two important pack-horse roads, it was originally called Barngates Inn. Perhaps it did not get a lot of visitors in those days, but whatever the reason, the story goes that a landlord found several barrels of ale had gone off and emptied the contents into a tarn close by the inn. His ducks, finding that the water had suddenly become more palatable than slugs and worms, slurped it down with gusto. Later that day, the landlord came out to find them hiccuping and so drunk they could not stand on their feet. Amused by this story, a later landlord changed the name of the inn to the Drunken Duck.

Early on Monday morning I phoned Border Television and Paul Murricain, a producer, came down with a film crew. He bubbled with enthusiasm about my journey and, with Thor and Jewel peering over his shoulders, trying to chew the end of the microphone, I described where we had been. The film crew gave the thumbs up to indicate they had got what they wanted and they all roared away in a big Volvo.

Selina had told me about an instructor at Brathay, called Dave England, who had done a six-month walking tour through Patagonia, carrying his equipment on a pack-pony. He sounded a really interesting chap and I went to see if I could find him. He was tied up with a course, but invited me to have dinner at the hall that evening and afterwards look through a collection of slides taken during his journey.

Returning to my campsite I found Selina and a friend, Liza, waiting for me. They had got the use of a Wayfarer sailing dinghy and wanted me to go out with them. I had not sailed for ages and was quite excited as we nosed out of the harbour, but there was hardly any wind and the surface of the lake was like a mirror. An occasional zephyr took the wrinkles out of the sails and created a gurgling wake as we surged ahead, but it soon died and we bobbed up and down in the wash of passing launches like a discarded detergent bottle. We drifted towards the centre of the lake and as if at a signal the sky darkened and it started to drizzle. Encouraged by the lack of opposition from the wind the clouds became bolder and opened the valves a bit more until the drizzle became a deluge and within minutes we were all drenched to the skin. While Liza steered and I stowed the sails, Selina paddled like a demon for the jetty, but there was no escape from the wetting. Approaching the boathouse there was something vaguely familiar about two objects sitting on the jetty, spilling over with water, and as we drew near I remembered they were my boots; I had kicked them off as I climbed into the dinghy.

Clutching my watery footwear, I slopped across to the tent and raising a nice fug with the primus stove, peeled off the wet layers and sanded yards of goose pimples with a rough towel. Wrapped in my spare clothes the blood began to circulate again, but footwear was a problem, I had only one pair of boots. Tying my wet clothes in a bundle I padded barefooted up to Selina's cottage and hung them in her drying room. Taking pity on my frozen feet, she lent me a pair of wellingtons and wearing these, a tatty pair of trousers and an embarrassingly evil-smelling sweater, I joined Dave England for dinner, in the smart surroundings of the dining room at Brathay Hall. Dave's slides of his journey through Patagonia were superb, though he had experienced all the problems of balancing the pack-saddle that had plagued me. The South American pack-saddle he had used was even more primitive than mine, but gave no problems. We spent a long time talking and drinking coffee and it was the early hours of the morning before I crawled into the tent.

CHAPTER 13

Onwards into Dunnerdale

I woke up to a beautiful fresh morning with the sun streaming through the trees and the surface of the lake a delicate blue. It was so quiet and still that I felt guilty about breaking the silence with the roar of the primus stove, but I wanted to make an early start and go through Grizedale Forest to Torver, near Coniston. Selina was going to come with me on her pony, then get a lift back in the evening.

A hot sun was already melting the tarmac as we emerged from the soft paths of the Brathay Estate onto the hard road. The morning rush of cars was building up, but we turned into a quiet by-road to Wray Castle and left them behind. Selina's little dog, Puddle, trotted at her side and our odd procession made its way along the country road, through sleepy hamlets, like a group of travelling pedlars of a century

As we passed the cluster of cottages at High Wray I wondered which one was the scene of a macabre justice, when on 8 April 1672, a certain Thomas L,

> who for poysoning his owne family was adjudged att the Assizes att Lancaster to bee carried back to his owne house att Hye Wray where hee lived, and was there hanged before his owne door till hee was dead, then was brought with a horse into Caulthouse Meadow and forthwith hung upp in iron chaynes on a gibbet which was sett for that very purpose on the South side of Sawrey near unto the Pooll Stang and there continued until the time as hee rotted.

Twisting down through the old Quaker settlement of Colthouse, the road levelled out and crossed Pool Bridge to Hawkshead. The heat was fierce and I could have made short work of something long and cool, but the tiny village was so crammed with people and cars we were glad to get away from it and climb the long steep hill towards Satterthwaite. At the top of the hill a large sign welcomed us to Grizedale Forest and it was a relief to turn off into the cool shade of tall spruce.

A maze of forestry roads shooting off in all directions rather upset our map reading and although the Forestry Commission had carried out quite a lot of route marking of paths, they had not got around to the bridleway to Parkamoor. Selina had ridden it the previous year, but meantime Forestry Commission bulldozers had made a few alterations to the landscape. We floundered around for a time until she recognized landmarks that put us on the right track and we jogged on and on through avenues of conifers until the road finally petered out in a bog, thickly overhung with trees. Dismounting, we led the ponies along a badly neglected path full of nasty looking holes and awkward clumps of grass. This section was probably about half a mile in length, but it seemed longer and I was greatly cheered when the sun broke through the trees and a gate appeared ahead, at the edge of the forest. The joy was short-lived, however, for as we got closer we discovered that a fence had been erected across the bridleway in front of the gate and there was absolutely no way through. Having come this far, I was in no mood for turning back, so out came the pliers and we cut through the netting and rolled it back. Fencing is expensive and I do not particularly enjoy damaging it, but until it is driven home to the authorities that the first essential of a National Park is unobstructed rights of way, landowners will continue to erect fences where they should not and the likes of me will have to cut holes in them.

Making sure the fence was carefully wired back into position, we left the shelter of the forest and rode out into the blinding sun. A thin path followed a winding route along a heathery plateau high above Coniston Water and the view was fantastic. The great mass of Coniston Old Man, Swirl How and Wetherlam shimmered in a deep blue haze, like a vast Impressionist painting hung in the sky. Tiny boats, with sails bright red and white, darted about the surface of the lake, then lay motionless, as a draught of rising air, warmed by the sun, drove them forward for a brief moment, then was gone.

Away from the patches of heather the ground was very wet and we made numerous long detours before we reached the isolated farmhouse of Parkamoor. I was filled with nostalgia as I rode into the yard and looked at the old house that held so many pleasant memories for me. When the National Trust acquired the property in 1968 I was their first tenant, but, despite the land having been farmed for generations, they argued it was not viable and let it off to neighbouring farmers. Built into the fell top, eight hundred feet above sea level, the house is reputed to be one of the oldest farmouses in the Lake District and when I lived there, local people told me all sorts of fascinating stories about the earlier tenants riding on horseback to Coniston for their groceries. There was one occasion when a local doctor was called to the house one fierce winter's night and ended up performing an appendix operation on the kitchen table, by the light of a candle. Writing in 1864, a Mr Gibson recorded that the hearth fire at Parkamoor had not been extinguished for centuries. There were certain superstitions attached to keeping fires going, in the old days, but from my experience of that beautifully situated, but very exposed, homestead, it is likely the fire was kept in for no other reason than to keep warm.

Selina held the ponies while I took a few photographs of the house, then we joined a good track that contoured round the steep flanks of Selside before dipping down to the road by Nibthwaite. At Water Yeat, where the River Crake pours out of Coniston Water on its way to the sea at Greenodd, we crossed a stone bridge and came out on the main Coniston to Ulverston road. There were a lot of cars about, but the drivers were very considerate as they passed by and, for once, I actually enjoyed riding along a road. A mile or so brought us to Brown Howe and we left the main road to follow a minor one as it climbed in and out of a wilderness of rock and bracken to Stable Harvey Farm. At the farm the bridlepath took to the open fell and crossed Stable Harvey Moss and, by a little tarn on Low Torver Common, to Beck Stones. Behind the old mill a wide cart track ran alongside a fast running beck, then swung through meadow land to cross the main road at Torver village and on between rows of cottages to Crook Farm. Selina knew the owners of the farm and in no time the ponies were in a field, the tent pitched in a sheltered hollow, and we were in the local pub, drinking iced lager that hardly touched the sides as it went down.

Later that evening a car load of friends arrived to take Selina back to Brathay. I was sorry to see her go. A strange, deep girl, not easy to get to know, but I had enjoyed her company enormously.

I slept heavily that night and when a crowing cock informed the world it was time to get up I was reluctant to leave my sleeping-bag. My muscles ached from the previous long day in the saddle and I lay back and soaked up the warm sun seeping through the thin canvas of the tent. The day seemed set to be another scorcher and the heavy dew had evaporated quicker than a political manifesto after a general election.

Clambering out into the warm air, I went down to the field for Thor and Jewel, but it took a good half hour before I managed to haul them out of ankle-deep grass. A few days of eating that luscious stuff and they would have been rolling about with bellyache, they would not be convinced though and sulked like a pair of children as I loaded up. Jewel had a little tantrum and refused to co-operate by puffing out her sides each time I tried to fasten the pack-saddle girth. I brought my knee sharply up into her flank and there was a hiss like a broken gas main as she expelled the air.

While I was busy tying the bags on, an old chap with a dog came by and he stopped to admire the ponies. We got to talking about local history and he told me there was once a pack-horse inn at Torver, but only the foundations were visible nowadays. I asked him how old the local church was.

'I don't know nowt about that,' he replied, 'but me grandfather used to tell a good tale about one of the parsons. He'd newly come to live in the dale and, not liking the way the wedding book had become worn and dog-eared, he bought a new one and put it in the vestry. Well, the next wedding they had in the church happened to be a widow marrying again, and when the time came to sign the wedding book the old parson was right put out to find the old book on the table, instead of the new one he had bought. After the wedding he asked where the new book had got to.

'"Oh," said the clerk, "I thought we'd keep the new book for virgins and the old one will do for the second time round 'uns."'

The Walna Scar road, used for centuries by the pack-horse trade and quarrymen working the bleak outcrops of slate, climbed away from Crook Farm, between high stone walls and under clumps of old sycamore, to the farmstead of Tranearth and the open fell. The wide path was deeply eroded above Tranearth and amongst the slag heaps and flooded pits of the disused Bannishead Quarry, the ponies were lathered in sweat as they fought to get a grip on the surface of broken shale. Above the quarry the path zigzagged up a steep slope of smooth grass and mercifully levelled out to join a broad stony track coming from the direction of Coniston. The bright sun disappeared as we crossed a traditional narrow pack-horse bridge spanning the rushing waters of Torver Beck and a long bank of cloud poured over Dow Crag, plunging the fells into a grey gloom. It became unbearably hot and humid, with hardly any air and the ponies barely managed to put one foot in front of the other with the effort of forcing themselves up the side of Brown Pike. I could almost hear them sigh with relief when we reached the top and looked down into Dunnerdale, so I eased the girths and let them snatch at the thin grass for a few minutes. The descent into Dunnerdale was easy at first, but lower down the path deteriorated into a quagmire of mud, churned up by tracture tyres and animals. By Long House Gill the mud gave way to a gully of spiky rocks but the worst was over and a bridge, cleverly constructed from slate, led onto a surfaced road.

Tying the ponies to a fence in the shade of a tree, I stretched out on the dry grass and listened to the music of the beck, tumbling and splashing over the rocks. The mountain fragrance of sheep and cows drifted up from the fields in the warm air, and a thrush in a nearby tree sang a love duet with his mate across the other side of the valley. It was blissfully peaceful and I dozed undisturbed, while on the other side of the fells the world tore along at an unhealthy pace, pushing and struggling in the ever increasing race for money and possessions.

An hour or so passed before the impatient stamping of the ponies roused me and I looked up to find them twitching manes and tails in a vain effort to dislodge swarms of persistent flies. The clouds had miraculously disappeared and the deep, wooded valley was bathed in brilliant sunlight. Preferring the shelter of the trees, the flies abandoned Thor and Jewel and we made our way, in sweltering heat, down the narrow road to the cluster of cottages and welcoming door of the Newfield Inn, at Seathwaite. I could have soaked up a very large glass of lager and lime, but British licensing laws make no allowance for thirsty travellers and the door was tightly closed. A wooden building next to the hotel displayed a battered sign advertising teas, so I went in. A cheerful girl served me and, as there was no one else waiting, she chatted for a while. It turned out she was the wife of a landlord of the Newfield Inn and she told me an intriguing tale about an incident years before, which the newspapers headlined as 'The Newfield Riot'.

The building in which I was enjoying a pot of tea was built in the early 1900s for the purpose of supplying stronger liquid to the gangs of navvies working on a dam, at Seathwaite Tarn, high in the fells on the Dunnerdale side of Dow Crag. According to local stories, they were a hard drinking bunch, and on pay days swarmed down to the Newfield and drank themselves into a stupor. The only way the contractor could get them back to work was to hire men with dogs to herd them up the road like sheep. The bar of the Newfield was too small to cope with such a crowd and the wooden building was erected to cater for them. After one particulary wild drinking session in July 1904, things got out of hand and they were evicted into the road. The drunken mob was in an ugly mood and attacked the building with stones and anything they could lay their hands on, smashing every window in the place. Breaking down the door of the inn, they surged forward and the landlord, in desperation, fired a shotgun into the mob, killing one man and seriously injuring another. Reports say it took the police two days to get to the scene from Broughton, about six miles away, but with that sort of reception waiting for him, the local constable could hardly be blamed for lack of enthusiasm as he pedalled his bicycle slowly up the Duddon valley

On the other side of the river, almost opposite the Newfield, was High Wallowbarrow, the home of Alan Ellwood and Jewel, but I could not find a shallow place to cross and we were forced to make a long detour, down to Hall

Dunnerdale and over Hall Bridge, before we could reach the farm.

Near Low Wallowbarrow Cottage an enormous billy-goat, with thick curved horns, advancing down the middle of the road, lowering his head as he came straight for us. Disturbed by the villainous look on his face, I kicked my feet out of the stirrups, ready for an unhindered blast off the saddle. Jewel, sensing danger, dropped back quickly, hiding behind Thor's tail. Normally Thor wants to climb over the nearest wall at the first hint of trouble, but this time he lumbered into battle like a war-horse. Billy arched his back ready to unleash the pair of scimitars perched on his head and that was enough for me. In a flash I cleared the saddle and was over the gate into the field as the two noses touched. Lying on the ground I waited for the explosion, but nothing happened. I peered through the gate and there stood a big, daft Fell pony and a heavily armed billy-goat rubbing their heads together and snuggling up like a couple of purring kittens. Jewel came out from the shelter of Thor's large backside and the three of them stood, heads together, nodding and snickering like a trio of old ladies discussing village gossip. I climbed back into the saddle, but Thor wouldn't budge. In the end, I had to get down and haul the bleating billy into a field and bang the gate shut, before we could continue on up to the farm.

Alan was out, mending a wall gap, but Peggy, his wife, showed me a field where I could pitch the tent. When I turned the ponies loose, Jewel careered around the field, with Thor after her, as though she was showing him where she lived. I went up to the house and Peggy produced a mug of tea and some cake. We got onto the subject of dry stone walls and how they were built in some peculiar places. Peggy talked about the days when she was a girl on the family farm in Langdale and how the farmers prided themselves on having neat walls. I said I could not understand how they managed to lift many of the enormous stones they used in some of the walls. Nowadays, if a wall fell down it often needed a tractor with a loader to lift the stones back. Peggy summed it up rather nicely when she replied, 'Ah well, they've lost the mould they used to make those fellows out of.'

When the sun sank behind Wallowbarrow Crag the midges came out in droves and sent me running for the tent. They poured in their thousands through the fine mesh of the ventilators and I had to keep the primus stove running to drive them away. When I let it out to go to sleep, they were back in force and I had to pull the sleeping-bag over my head to escape the torment.

CHAPTER 14

Near Tragedy in Mosedale

The night was hot and uncomfortable and next morning I awoke to a horrifying sight. I had unconsciously worked myself out of the sleeping-bag and, as it was far too hot to sleep with anything on, all was exposed. During the night a seething mass of 'women's libbers', reincarnated as midges, had attacked with uncontrolled ferocity that masculine appendage my youngest daughter politely refers to as a 'gentleman's willy'. Such was the carnage, the poor thing had swollen to three times its normal size. I would have been full of admiration were it not for the pain, and that was absolutely excruciating. No matter which way I turned, I could not find a comfortable position. The burning pain was so intense I resorted to the time-honoured way of reducing it by filling my drinking mug with cold water and lowering the fiery willy into the soothing depths. If you have ever plunged a red-hot poker into a bucket of water you will know the reaction. Phew! The relief was indescribable. The problem was what to do now. I could hardly ride with a mug of water balanced on the saddle, besides I needed it for my coffee. I solved it by cocooning the injured organ in a thick layer of vaseline and hauling my jeans gingerly above my knees, I managed to make breakfast.

It took me a long time to strike camp and get the ponies ready for leaving. A searing pain shot through me at every movement and the simple chore of packing each bag and weighing it with the spring balance became a major operation.

Leaving Wallowbarrow we clambered up the stony path

twisting through a wood, to the foot of Wallowbarrow Crag, then slanting upwards close by the remote farmstead of Stonythwaite. Since early morning the sun had hung high in the sky and from a rosy glow had developed into a blistering ball of fire, bleaching the grass and making the trees droop in the unaccustomed heat. The rocks by the side of the path were so hot you could almost have fried an egg on them.

On the open fell there was not a scrap of shelter where we could get away from the harsh sun and the sweat poured off Thor and Jewel as they slogged along the high path between Stonythwaite and Grassguards, at the edge of Dunnerdale Forest. Sensing Grassguards Gill they surged forward, eager to taste the cool water. Hidden from the sun, behind the wall of a barn at Grassguards, the air smelt of damp moss and soil and I relaxed in the shade, watching the expression of relief spread over the ponies' faces as they stood knee deep in a clear pool and drank their fill.

Around my nether regions the mystical powers of the vaseline were beginning to take effect and the pain subsided. At first I thought the tortured instrument might have fallen off, but a quick glance assured me all was well. I felt a lot happier as I climbed into the saddle and pressed Thor along a grassy path, into the silence of the forest. Out of the sun the ponies were a lot livelier and we jogged at a comfortable pace along a soft carpet of moss, between musky conifers. Whatever critics have to say against coniferous trees, as far as I am concerned, no mountain scenery would be complete without them. They have the same rugged beauty and indifference to the vagaries of our unfriendly climate as the very mountains themselves, and are an essential part of the landscape. When I worked for the Forestry Commission in Scotland, I met a visitor one day, who thought it disgraceful that trees not native to the country were grown in large numbers. He argued that there was too much foreign influence in this country and nothing should be tolerated unless its origin was truly British. While he rambled on I noticed that the binoculars round his neck were German, his camera was made in Japan and his walking boots were imported from Austria. Somehow his argument did not make sense.

'Emerging from the wood the path sloped down to Birks Farm and crossed the yard to a field gate. We were almost through when a loud whinny echoed across the field and a huge Clydesdale came thundering over to meet us. Standing seventeen hands high, he towered above the Fell ponies and, though he rubbed his great head admiringly against Jewel's neck, he did not take to Thor and lashed at him with feet the size of dinner plates. When I tried to get Thor into the field, the big fellow whipped round and an enormous iron-shod hoof whizzed past my head, shattering the top rail of the gate. Retreating hurriedly, I let Thor stand while I led Jewel away from the gate, luring the great heap of Scottish horseflesh behind her. With Thor safely across, I collected Jewel and, leaving the Clydesdale charging about the field with frustration, we dived down the path to the River Duddon and Birks Bridge.

Underneath the ancient pack-horse bridge, countless centuries of water rushing down from the fells had gouged a deep cleft in the rock and, in the bright sunlight, the swift river boiled and tumbled in glistening cascades into the crystal clear pools. The water was very inviting as we crossed the bridge, but I knew if we stopped it would not be easy to get going again. Beyond Birks Bridge was open country and, without hobbles, I would soon have to find a place to camp for the night where there was a field to graze the ponies.

A few yards up the road by the Forestry Commission's car park a neglected bridlepath followed a marshy route, between the river and the forest fence, through a coppice of silver birch, to a gate leading into a field. A small herd of black Galloway cattle with their calves grazed peacefully on the fresh grass, but moved obligingly to one side as we approached. All but one, that is, and that one had a ring in his nose. With head lowered and foreleg pawing the ground, he was not actually welcoming us to his field, but as Thor got nearer the brute backed off and glowered as we hurried by. I spurred Thor for a distant gate , but Mr Galloway was not to be put off. With a loud bellow, half a ton of beefsteak came thundering after us, tail in the air and in no mood for games. Lashing Thor into action, I sped towards the river, Jewel racing behind, with the swaying pack threatening to snap every lashing. At the fence I did not stop to look back and cleared it in one dive. It was not a second too soon. A horrible black head loomed over the fence, snorting and drooling and I stared into a pair of mean red eyes, wild with fury at being stopped by a strand of barbed wire. He butted the fence repeatedly, but it eventually penetrated his thick skull that he could not reach me, and, roaring with rage, he raced back to his harem. Incredibly, he ignored the ponies and they grazed contentedly as if nothing had happened.

For a number of years there have been differences of opinion in the Lake District, about whether bulls should be allowed in fields through which there is a public right of way. How it should be resolved is difficult to say, but if those who insist that a bull is not a potentially dangerous animal had joined me over the fence and shared my elastoplast, they may well have changed their views.

Clear of the field we squelched along a churned up path to the firm meadows of Black Hall Farm. The farm is also a youth hostel, but there was not a soul about as I led the ponies through the well trodden earth of the yard and along the track leading to Cockley Beck. At Cockley Beck Farm I knocked on the door to ask if I could camp, but there was no reply. Like the folk at Black Hall, they were probably away at a sale, so I lay back in the soft grass by the beckside, watching convoys of sunbaked motor cars, packed with sweating passengers and panting dogs, cross the bridge and climb with protesting engines towards Hardknott Pass.

Cockley Beck is one of the remotest communities in the Lake District and, in winter, probably the bleakest. Years ago there were many more small farms in upper Dunnerdale, all struggling to scratch a living from the shallow soil and old records of fines, imposed for allowing sheep to stray, show how important each blade of grass was to the survival of a family. Usually, the only educated man in these areas was the parson and he looked after his flock like a true patriarch. The best known of all the country parsons was Robert Walker, who lived at Gaitskill in Dunnerdale in the eighteenth century and was an incredibly active man. Known far and wide as 'Wonderful Walker', he not only preached the gospel and taught at the village school, but somehow found time to act as parish clerk, spin wool and brew beer for sale, and hire himself out as a labourer during sheep-shearing and harvest. Obviously thriving on hard work, he was Vicar of Seathwaite for sixty-six years and died in 1802, at the ripe old age of ninety-three.

The afternoon was advancing and there was no sign of anyone at the farm, so I decided to press on through Mosedale and camp at Throstle Garth, at the head of Eskdale, where the powerful Lingcove Beck merges with the young Esk and helps it to attain the status of a river. I knew there was a good sheep-pen near the beck where I could put the ponies for the night.

Like so many of the ancient pack-horse routes, the path up Mosedale was firm and dry at first, and, although it was unbearably hot, the ponies had no difficulty following a well worn route by the side of Mosedale Beck. As we climbed higher the long ridge of Scafell Pike filled the head of the valley and I knew it would not be long before Thor and Jewel would be nibbling the close-cropped grass beside the impressive waterfalls of Lingcove Beck. The rough surface of the path gave way to soft turf and finally petered out altogether at the edge of a wide expanse of bog, spread right across the valley. It was no worse than we had encountered at other times and I led the ponies higher up the fellside to firmer ground. It was heavy going, clambering over large tufts of grass and rock, and Thor and Jewel were gasping before we had gone half a mile. Leaving them by a boulder, I went ahead to test the ground. It was very wet in patches, but seemed firm enough when I jumped up and down on it. Ahead I could see dry bracken-covered ground, and once we reached it we would be safe; but it was not to be.

We had only gone a few yards when Jewel, heavily laden with the pack, broke through the surface and sank up to her belly in a slimy bog. Desperately trying to flounder through, the heat and the effort were too much and she keeled over and lay on her side. Frantically I cut through the girth strap and dragged the pack and saddle off her back, but she lay perfectly still, with not a twitch of a muscle or any sign that she was breathing. I lifted her eyelids, but they fell back lifeless, and, putting my ear to her side, there was not even the merest flutter of a heartbeat. Tearing my spare shirt out of the pack, I ran to a beck and soaked it in the icy water. For two hours I sponged Jewel's hot body, running to and fro from the beck, when the shirt dried in the heat, but my efforts seemed in vain. It looked as if Jewel was dead. I returned to the beck for one more try with cold water and as I squeezed it on to her face, to my intense joy, she opened her eyes and tried to sit up. I was so relieved I hugged her to me and gave her a huge kiss. For an hour she sat on her haunches like a dog and all the time I talked to her and sponged her down, hoping she would try to eat. When an animal loses its will to live nothing can save it and I was afraid Jewel may have been pushed too far. If I could get her to eat she would be on the road to recovery. Free from the weight of the pack she managed to stagger to her feet and I coaxed her out on to firm ground. She stood for a while, then snatched at the rough grass. I cannot describe the feeling of utter pleasure and relief that swept over me as I stood with Jewel by that awful bog and listened to her crunching grass. There is no money in the world that could equal such an experience and in comparison the oil sheikhs are paupers.

Fortunately, Thor had the sense not to wander while I was busy tending to Jewel and I led them back down the valley to safe ground. Ferrying the bags and harness down to the ponies was hot, tedious work and although it was getting on for seven o'clock in the evening the fierce sun showed no sign of relenting. Jewel rested while I repaired the girth and seemed no worse for her ordeal when I buckled the harness onto her back. To reduce the weight I divided the load and lashed as much as I could on to Thor's saddle.

There was still no one at Cockley Beck Farm, so I walked the ponies up to the foot of Hardknott Pass, hoping to find a campsite. There was a nice soft patch of grass to pitch the tent on, by the side of Hardknott Gill, but nowhere I could safely keep the ponies for the night. I felt weary and depressed as I sat working out what I should do, but the antics of the motorists trying to drive up the first steep section of the pass soon cheered me up.

A car ran up the one in three incline almost to the first bend, paused, then hurtled backwards down again, thudding into the grass bank a few feet away from where I sat. Engine revving furiously, it lurched forward for another attempt. Up it climbed again, almost to the first bend, then stalled. The doors flew open and white-faced passengers poured out, leaving the driver to his fate. Swerving all over the road, with smoke pouring from his brake-drums, he backed down and crashed neatly into the hole he had made in the bank on his first attempt. The poor man sat at the wheel shaking, and as soon as his passengers had trudged down to join him, started his engine and returned down the road to Cockley Beck. The next car had an even more hilarious variation of the theme. Having failed twice to get past the first bend, he gave the engine full throttle and, wheels screeching on gravel, roared up again. I almost cheered as he rounded the bend, but he tried to change gear, missed it and jerked to a halt. The doors opened and his passengers baled out, but meantime he found his gear and shot away, too scared to stop, with three portly ladies shouting after him. He disappeared round the hairpin bends, pursued by his women and I lost sight of them. Perhaps it was the chance he had been waiting for.

Looking at the map I realized that Brotherilkeld Farm, in Eskdale, was only a short distance away on the other side of Hardknott Pass. They allowed camping on their land and we could be there in an hour or so. I checked the lashing on Thor's packs and, with Jewel fully recovered to her normal perky self, we plodded up the tortuous pass, overtaken at frequent intervals by startled motorists, surprised to find two pack-ponies where they rightly belonged. If the occupants of those brightly painted metal monsters did but know it, the horse had carried goods and people over Hardknott Pass for hundreds of years and it was the last route to be regularly used by the pack-horse gangs, before wheeled transport finally ousted them from the Lake District forever.

The locals tell a grand story about a character who used to travel over Hardknott Pass with a gang of pack-horses, plying between Kendal and Whitehaven. He rode a pony and, being rather fond of his ale, had a habit of dashing ahead of his pack-horse to an inn, where he would sit drinking until they had passed, led by an old black stallion who probably knew the way better than anybody. A few more drinks and he would overtake them again and wait at the next inn. Apparently he did this all the way to

Whitehaven, but whether he managed to ride back to Kendal, or was carried, history does not record.

At the top of the pass we rested and I sat on a rock, mesmerized by an amazing sunset. Way down the long green valley of Eskdale, far beyond Ravenglass, the blue spire of the ancient kingdom of the Isle of Man hung suspended above a glistening sea, framed by vivid shafts of golden light from the dying sun. It was as if the Norse gods had returned in a blaze of glory, beckoning the souls of the early Viking marauders to their final resting-place in the great Valhalla. The last chords of the glorious symphony of light reached a vibrating crescendo in the evening sky and the mystic island faded into the purple horizon. A snort from Thor brought me back to earth and I looked round to find he had somehow managed to get tangled up in his lead rope and was having his neck stretched.

Descending into Eskdale we had to take great care on the smooth tarmac. The spinning tyres of countless cars had left a coating of rubber on each bend and I had one heart-stopping moment when both ponies skied down a particularly greasy section and slid to a halt on the brink of a long drop into the valley. Below the hairpin bends the road levelled out and dipped gently towards the ruin of Hardknott Fort. Built by the Romans, it commands an impressive position and in summer, must have been what estate agents glowingly describe as a 'highly desirable residence, with uninterrupted views over unspoilt country-side'. Winter would be a different story. The Roman soldiers, fresh from the land of the sun, probably cursed Cumberland as the worst place on earth, as they paced the battlements, frozen to their spears, with a westerly gale whistling up their togas.

Reaching Brotherilkeld we toiled wearily up to the farmhouse and I asked permission to camp. Eric Harrison, the tenant, looked very embarrassed and explained that he had recently been stopped from taking campers, by the National Trust, who owned the farm. It was a terrible blow. The next farm which allowed camping was miles down the valley and it would be dark before we got anywhere near it. The ponies looked very dejected as they stood patiently in the farmyards and, with a true farmer's appreciation of how they were feeling, Eric blurted out, 'Oh, to hell with it! Those ponies are about done in. Put your tent in the field and let them have a good rest.'

I stayed for two days while Thor and Jewel rolled the aches from their muslces and mowed the sweet grass. The weather was unbearably hot, driving me out of the oven-like tent each morning, to lie gasping in the shade of a tree. My small stock of margarine, chocolate and candles melted into a revolting runny mess, but I could not afford to throw it away and I was never quite sure which I was eating.

Checking the ponies, I discovered that Jewel had lost a shoe. I could not find it anywhere in the field and, maybe in the distant future a workman will pick it up in Mosedale, during the excavation of drains for a row of new council houses stretching from Cockley Beck to Scafell Pike. On the telephone the local blacksmith was very helpful and said he would make a new shoe and meet me at Brantrake in two days' time.

CHAPTER 15

Brotherilkeld to Brantrake

It was so hot in the tent I had difficulty in sleeping and seemed to have dozed only for a few minutes when a cockerel leapt on to a nearby gate and crowed 'wakey wakey' with such irritating monotony I flung a boot at him. The pest shot away with a loud squawk and a flurry of feathers, but there was no point in returning to my sleeping-bag. After breakfast I hauled everything out of the tent with the intention of making an early start, but having spent much of the morning talking to the Harrisons, the day was well advanced when I rode Thor down to Wha House bridge and a gate leading into a tree-lined meadow. The old pack-horse road crossed the meadow to a wood and on through bracken, so tall at times the ponies were out of sight under it. Crossing the boulder-strewn beck, the track improved, following a well-worn route through pasture land and numerous gates, to Penny Hill Farm. In the days when pack-horses and droves of cattle passed by from Ravenglass, the farm was an inn called Pyet's Nest. It would be a popular resting-place with the drovers before they tackled Hardknott Pass and, doubtless, the pack-horse man on the pony drank many a tankard of ale there, as his animals trooped through the yard led by the black stallion.

On the opposite side of the river from Penny Hill I could see a large marquee in the grounds of Eskdale Youth Hostel and went to see what was happening. A long line of expensive cars were parked around the building and, in a sweat-stained shirt and ragged jeans, I stuck out like a sore thumb among a throng of smartly dressed people, scattered about the lawn. Jeff Lee, the warden, was his usual cheery self.

'You've just arrived in time,' he cried, as I walked through the front door, 'grab a plate and tuck in. There's a lot left over.'

In the hostel common-room a row of tables groaned under a vast array of sandwiches, sausage rolls, scones, fancy cakes and other mouth-watering delicacies. While I loaded a plate, Jeff explained that Edward Short, MP, had officially opened a new hostel extension and the ceremony had been followed by a buffet lunch. Having been reduced to almost subsistence level over the past few weeks, the sight of unlimited free food roused the animal instinct in me. I bolted down sandwiches and rolls and returned to the table to fill up on jam tarts, cream cakes, marshmallows and biscuits. Jeff's wife, Ann, brought a large pot of tea and I washed the food down with cup after cup, until I was so full I could hardly move. Filling a large bag with cream cakes for the ponies, I thanked the Lees and set off back to Penny Hill. A battle royal raged in my distended stomach, with *pâté* rolls and cucumber taking great exception to being showered with cream and sticky jam. Unaccustomed to such rich food, I felt decidedly queasy. Thor and Jewel chomped greedily at the cakes and all along the bridleway, past Doctor Bridge and Low Birker Farm, they sucked and slurped at a thick layer of cream stuck to their faces.

Near Dalegarth the tiny church of St Catherine appeared through the trees and I rode down to the river and crossed a ford to have a look at it. The attractive little building, with its twin bell tower, is a typical dales church, built low to withstand fierce weather and enclosed by a stout wall of local stone. Scattered about the churchyard, weather-beaten headstones unfolded a story of the local people as good as any history book. The lack of proper medical facilities and the poverty of the early agricultural communities was evident from many graves of young people and sometimes whole families. Headstones of farmers and their families from Wasdale Head were a grim reminder of the harsh days when the final journey of the inhabitants of that lonely place was made on the back of a pony, over the wild expanse of Burnmoor, to Eskdale.

Nestling in peaceful solitude on the banks of the quiet flowing River Esk, it is hard to imagine that the church was founded as the result of a drunken orgy. A group of French and English noblemen, including William de Etheling, son of Henry I, and Richard, Earl of Chester, had been strengthening Anglo-French relationships with a drinking session in a French port. To round off the evening's merriment, they ordered the captain of the good ship, *Blanche Nif*, to set sail for England, but, hardly had they cleared the harbour, when the ship was driven onto rocks and all on board were lost. Ranulph Meschines, the first Earl of Carlisle, succeeded to the Earldom of Chester and, being a deeply religious man, founded the church in Eskdale, naming it St Catherine's in memory of his kinsman, who perished in the ship on St Catherine's Day, 1120.

While I wandered among the headstones Thor and Jewel saved the verger a job, by trimming the grass round the edge of the church wall, and were not at all happy about leaving it unfinished, when I hauled them away up the track to Dalegarth Hall. It was dark and cool under the tall trees of Low Wood and the sun seemed even hotter when we crossed the open meadows by Milkingstead.

The piercing shriek of a whistle echoed across the valley and through the trees behind Fisherground Farm a tiny steam-engine of the Ravenglass and Eskdale railway appeared, puffing and wheezing under the strain of hauling a long line of coaches packed with excited youngsters. Over the years the attractive little railway has provided a valuable service and given pleasure to many thousands of people, but although it chugs along today with a reasonably secure future, there were times when the hands running along the engines were not those of fond admirers, but scrap merchants assessing their value in the melting-pot.

It all started in 1871 with the formation of a company called Whitehaven Iron Mines Ltd, who planned to operate a mine at Boot in Eskdale. Taking the ore from the mine to Ravenglass by horse and cart would have been costly and time consuming, so a railway company was formed and a three-foot gauge line laid to link up with the Furness Railway. The railway company was independent of the mining company and opened for goods only in 1875. A year later it was licensed to carry passengers – and it was a rare luxury for a remote dale to have its own railway service. It must have been a great boon to farmers who had fertilizer and feedstuffs brought in by sea to Ravenglass. Oddly enough, despite the regular traffic of goods and passengers, the railway company went bankrupt only two years after it opened and a receiver was appointed. The Whitehaven Iron Mines Ltd, faced with the prospect of resorting to the horse and cart for carrying their ore, persuaded the receiver to keep the railway going, and incredibly it opened a branch line in 1880, at Beckfoot, to carry ore from a new mine across the Esk at Sill Force. Ironically, in 1882, Whitehaven Iron Mines Ltd went bust and it seemed the end of the railway.

By some miracle the company managed to scratch a living carrying granite and a new source of revenue, the tourist, right through into the new century. In 1908 the line was pronounced unsafe and the boiler fires were doused once more. A new company called the Eskdale Railway Company was formed. It struggled on for a while, carrying granite or iron ore, but finally came to a halt when Nab Gill mines at Boot were overwhelmed by floods. In April 1913 the valley lost its three-foot gauge railway for ever.

In 1915 W.J. Bassett-Lowke, the famous model engineer, was searching the country for a line on which to test his scale model locomotives when he heard about the derelict railway at Eskdale. He found it ideal for his purpose and having leased it he set about converting the line to fifteen-inch gauge. By 1916 services were running as far as Eskdale Green, and the line was eventually extended to the old mine station at Boot. The climb to the mine station caused the little engines to wheeze more than was good for them, so that stretch of line from Beckfoot was abandoned and the 1880 branch line used, finally to terminate at the present Dalegarth Station. The new miniature railway operated a regular service throughout the year, carrying goods, passengers and mail.

In 1922 the company received a welcome injection of cash when a local resident, Sir Aubrey Brocklebank, the shipping magnate, opened Beckfoot granite quarry and the railway carried a large tonnage of granite to the crushing plant at Murthwaite, then on to the main line at Ravenglass. At one time a standard gauge line was laid over the fifteen-inch line to enable goods wagons to load direct at Murthwaite.

In 1925, Henry Lithgow, another famous name in shipping, joined Sir Aubrey as a partner and they took over the railway company. Passenger traffic seems to have declined, for in 1927 the winter service was withdrawn and at the outbreak of the Second World War, passenger services were discontinued altogether. Traffic from the quarry continued during the war and when it was over, the summer passenger service was restored in 1946. On the death of Henry Lithgow in 1948, the railway was sold to the Keswick Granite Company, but in 1953 they decided the quarry at Beckfoot was uneconomical and it was closed down. The railway was offered for sale, but no attractive offers landed on the manager's desk so it was decided to put it up for auction on 7 September 1960.

A resident of Ravenglass, the late Douglas Robinson, saw that if nothing was done, the scrap merchants would at last descend like locusts, smashing, cutting and dismembering, and the only legacy of the great little railway would be poignant memories and seven miles of undisturbed grazing for the rabbits. A public appeal was launched and with the help of newspapers and radio, a surge of public interest was aroused and money came pouring in. Despite this wonderful response, only about half the asking price of £14,000 was realized and the auction day hovered like a cloud of doom. At the eleventh hour two saviours emerged in the form of Mr Colin Gilbert and Sir Wavell Wakefield (now Lord Wakefield of Kendal). These gentlemen offered to provide, not only the balance required for the purchase of the railway, but also as much again for working capital. This wonderful gesture saved the day, and Douglas Robinson experienced the thrill of making the successful final bid of £12,000 at the auction in Gosforth Village Hall. A company was formed under the chairmanship of Mr Gilbert, with Sir Wavell and a representative from the Preservation Society, as co-directors. Following the sad loss of Mr Gilbert, who died in 1968, Lord Wakefield acquired his interest and became chairman.

The Ravenglass and Eskdale Railway Preservation Society was the outcome of Douglas Robinson's appeal for public support. The railway company operate the day-to-day running of the railway under the direction of the General Manager, Mr Douglas Ferreira, and the Preservation Society support it by providing voluntary workers, and publicizing the railway throughout the country. The society's pride and joy is the steam engine, *River Mite*, which was built through their fund-raising efforts. Many improvements have taken place since the formation of the company. A new signal box has been built at Ravenglass and, in 1972, a really interesting acquisition appeared in the form of the Victorian awning which had, for years, sheltered passengers on the British Rail's station at Millom.

The railway is known far and wide as 'la-al Ratty'. There

are conflicting opinions as to the origin of the name, but Doug Ferreira has the most logical explanation. The contractor who built the original line in 1874 was a Mr Ratcliffe. More than likely, his men would nickname him 'Ratty' and the line would be jokingly referred to as 'Ratty's Railway'. Hence 'The Ratty'.

Beyond Milkingstead the track joined the tarmac road at Forge Bridge and on both sides, all the way to Brantrake, the tractors were cutting rectangular patterns in the ripe grass, wafting the sweet scent of new-mown hay across the fields as I pitched camp in the shade of a large hawthorn by Brantrake House. David and Rachel Sharp had departed to their farm, but a family on holiday from Edinburgh were very friendly and plied me with cans of lager. Turning the ponies into a field, I gratefully accepted an invitation to the house and spent a very pleasant evening with the Robinsons, yarning, long after darkness had crept over the woods and meadows of the silent valley.

CHAPTER 16

The Last Leg

I got up early the next morning, to photograph an interesting piece of Lakeland history, on the fell behind Brantrake. It was nothing more exciting than a hole in the ground, yet it had been dug with a special purpose in mind. About four feet in diameter and perhaps two feet deep, it was lined with blocks of stone, with provision for a wooden lid to fit over the top of it. I had known about it for years and thought it was a place where bygone tenants of Brantrake had kept food, to keep it cool in hot weather. Jack Porter, the Master of the Eskdale and Ennerdale Foxhounds, put me right. Looking furtively over his shoulder, as though expecting the arm of the law to descend at any minute, he had confided that it had been built many years ago, to put fighting cocks in, a day or so before a contest. In the evil days, when cockfighting was more popular than 'Match of the Day' with the dalesfolk, it was the custom to keep fighting cocks confined, so that when they were released, they were sufficiently peeved about the restriction to expend their venom on the first object that confronted them, usually the opposing bird.

Although the sport was highly illegal and the police often raided farms, the locals were too crafty for them and usually the place was empty when they arrived. Jack told me about a time when, as a young lad, he went with his father to a cockfight at a farm near Devoke Water, on Birker Fell. The contest was well under way when a look-out dashed in, shouting that a man in uniform was coming across the moor. There was pandemonium as the crowd rushed for the barn door and disappeared in all directions, trying to stuff squawling cockerels into bags as they ran. Half an hour later, when the farmer's wife nervously opened the door in response to a loud knock, she found it was only the postman.

The blacksmith arrived as I was packing the gear and by eleven o'clock we were making our way along the road towards Forge Bridge. In a big field by the King George IV clanking machines were busy scooping up mouthfuls of loose hay, ramming it into rectangular bales and ejecting them in neat lines ready for the trailer following behind. Soon the field would be echoing with the merriment of the annual dog show, when the hounds are brought back to the Eskdale Hunt Kennels from farms where they have been 'walked out' during the summer. Prizes are given for the best-kept dog, horn-blowing, singing and children's sports. It is always a well attended meeting, with much laughter and fun. I was once at a dog show in another part of the Lake District, when the announcer said, 'Now ladies and gentlemen, can I have your attention for the champion bitch.' At that moment, the large-busted figure of the wife of a local dignitary, well known for her sharp tongue, chose the wrong time to make her grand entrance into the ring. Instead of the hushed respect she had hoped for, the crowd howled with laughter for so long we missed seeing the poor animal who was the star of the show.

By Eskdale Green Station I hesitated. If I turned left I could be over Muncaster Fell and back to Ravenglass in an hour or so, but the thought of returning to civilization frightened me. For weeks I had been as close to nature as anyone could get. Free as the wind, to wander where the notion took me. Taking the weather as it came, asking nothing and dependent on no one. I could not bear the thought of going back. My foodstock was almost exhausted and I was down to my last pound, but beyond the trees was another valley, another range of fells and more forgotten trails of the pack-horse days. I pulled Thor back onto the road, determined to keep going as long as I could.

It was the hottest day yet and in the gutters tar from the road ran in black rivulets through the dust. Along the winding road we went, beneath the welcome shade of the huge trees, leaning out from the grounds of the Outward Bound School and out again into the merciless glare of the sun. The air was so hot it was painful to breathe and poor Thor laboured so badly I was forced to rest him by a large hedge at the foot of Mitredale. An elderly lady came by as I was busy sponging Thor down with a wet cloth and she stopped to admire the ponies.

'My,' she said, 'they's a fair pair of Fells. Fair takes me back to when I was a lass. Me father always kept five or six Fells on the farm and reckoned they could work in spots no big horse would ever dare go.' She walked round examining each pony closely. Lifting Thor's upper lip, she peered expertly at his teeth. 'This old lad's seen a few summers, but there's plenty of work left in him yet.'

I was wondering whether I should tell her about his ailments when she turned her attention to Jewel.

'A bonny pony, but a bit on the light side. That's what comes from messing about trying to breed for showing instead of working. Father wouldn't have had a pony on the place unless it had plenty of width in the shoulders and back.' Eyeing the pack-saddle, she went on, 'Eeh, Grandfather used to tell a tale or two about when they used to take stuff about on pack-ponies. In them days there were no roads like there is now and he, and his father, had to take their wool over the fells to Keswick. There's a place up Mitredale called the "Highway" but he used to frighten me sister and me to death with a tale about a murder at a farm up there. Every year I come back on holiday, but I've never plucked up courage to go and see the spot yet.'

I said that I had read somewhere that the old pack-horse route through Mitredale was, at one time, called the

'Highway', but I had not heard about the murder.

'I don't know that I believe it myself, mind,' she said unconvincingly, 'but Grandfather said that a young couple with a baby had a farm up by the head of the dale. The husband had to take some beasts to Whitehaven and, of course, in them days he would have to walk them all the way and come back next day. That night the wife was busy making candles from a tub of melted tallow when there was a knock on the door. She wasn't too keen to open it, but when she found it was only an old woman, wrapped in a hooded cloak and looking for shelter for the night, she took her into the kitchen and told her to go by the fire while she made her a bite to eat. The old woman seated herself in the open fireplace and fell fast asleep in the warmth. When the farm wife went to wake her for her supper she found that the cloak had slipped and, instead of an old woman, she saw an evil-looking man with a knife stuck in his belt. Terrified that the man would harm her or her child, in desperation, she took the bowl of hot tallow she had been making candles with and poured it into the man's mouth as he lay snoring. When the farmer returned the next day he found the man dead and his wife a blubbering wreck. Grandfather used to say that the body was buried under the cobbles of the farmyard, but he never said what happened to the farmer and his wife.'

Having listened to the old lady's gruesome story I was glad to leave the dark shade of the hedge and return to the heat of the sun. I half expected her to vanish into the air, pulling the hood of a cloak over her head, but instead she trotted merrily down the road in the direction of Irton Road Station.

As we passed the Bower House Inn a line of lunchtime drinkers sitting in the shade of the wall raised their pints of cool beer tantalizingly in salute, but I ignored the temptation and steered Thor up the long hill towards Santon Bridge. Both he and Jewel were white with sweat by the time we had reached the top, but there was not a drop of water to be found among the bleached rocks of the dried-up becks. I had filled a bottle with water before leaving Brantrake and I poured it into my riding hat and shared it between them. The heat was intense and every time we came to a large tree overhanging the road, we halted in the shade for a few minutes to escape from the fiery orb which threatened to reduce us to three grease spots on the road.

Looking across the valley during one of these brief escapes, I was infuriated to find that a rather nice house, which had recently been sold to a man who had retired to the area from a city, was already sprouting notices telling the world to 'Keep Out' and 'No Trespassing'. The message was helped along by rows of ugly barbed wire strewn about the fences and gates. The Lake District could well do without these sort of people. They contribute nothing to a community and their selfishness creates only unpleasantness and acrimony. The great Lakeland poet and writer, Norman Nicholson, summed up the breed magnificently when he wrote,

> There are two sorts of tourists; those who return and those who stay, and the latter are more destructive. There is a sort of man who can come into a district that is new to him and can take root there, can learn to accept its traditions, to adapt himself to its people, to assume, like the birds, lepidoptera, a protective colouring. But there is another who remains, all his life, a stranger, a foreigner, looking on from the outside, trying, perhaps unconsciously, to make the people and the land adapt themselves to him.

The road wound to a final crest beneath the tree-lined slopes of Irton Pike and, before descending to Santon Bridge, we rested beneath the cool larch, by a memorial stone to William Malkinson. This poor chap had succumbed to the effects of heat, but in a rather ironic way.

On a cold misty Sunday in February 1886, William Malkinson, a Wesleyan preacher, set out from Santon Bridge to take the service at a chapel in Eskdale. He had made the journey many times before and several locals saw him and returned his cheery greeting as he tramped up the steep hill and was swallowed up by the mist. In Eskdale, the congregation waited patiently on their hard benches for the preacher to appear, but, as time passed, they began to get worried for they knew William Malkinson would have set out whatever the weather. Finally a search party was got together and at the top of the hill, on the spot now marked by the stone, they found their preacher lying by the side of the road. A doctor was summoned from Gosforth, but by the time he arrived, on horseback, it was too late. William Malkinson was found to be wearing two heavy overcoats, two waistcoats, and two mufflers and, apparently, the heat generated by the exertion of climbing up the hill had brought on a seizure.

There was not a soul to be seen as we plodded through Santon Bridge and turned down the narrow road to Wasdale. Even the cows and sheep had abandoned the lush meadows and lay gasping in the shade of the hedgerows, plagued by millions of flies that lay in a thick mass over their heads and bodies. A farm dog climbed stiffly to his feet as we passed a yard gate and made as if to come after us, but in the heat the effort was too much and he contented himself with a threatening growl from beneath the cool shelter of a baler. Sweat dripped from the ponies like rain water as we toiled up the long hill by Greengate Wood and at the top I slacked off the girths and let them snatch at the coarse grass while I sucked the juice from an orange and gazed at the view. Beyond Flass Wood, the fertile fields of the lower valley gave way to the superb mountain panorama of Wasdale, swinging from the imposing Buckbarrow Crag on the north side, across the sharp edge of Yewbarrow to the friendly dome of

Great Gable, over Scafell and down the long ridge of Illgill Head, with its fantastic flutes of scree pouring into the cold depths of Wastwater. It is a view well known to many thousands of visitors to the Lake District and they return, year after year, to renew their passionate relationship, whether by lovingly tramping the familiar paths or simply staring, entranced, from the comfort of a car.

Returning to the ponies I found the pair of them sniffing warily at a poor frightened little vole, cowering in the grass and doing its best to pretend it did not exist. First Thor sniffed, then backed away, then Jewel did the same. To give each other courage they both sniffed together, then backed off, like inseparable Siamese twins. Having been bowled over a few times by rapidly exhaled horsy breath, the vole decided to make a run for it, just as the two noses came down for another joint sniff. With a squeak it shot into the long grass and the result was electrifying. Thor and Jewel jumped about six feet into the air and, given the chance, I am sure they would have swarmed up the nearest tree. 'You great pair of softies,' I said, as we rode down the hill towards Nether Wasdale.

The ponies sensed water as we approached Forest Bridge and soon their muzzles were thrust deep into the icy waters of the River Irt, that flows out of Wastwater to join the Esk and Mite in the harbour at Ravenglass. While they drank and splashed, I rested in the shade of the grey stone bridge and admired the workmanship of the stonemasons. In recent years the bridge had been widened for the benefit of the motor car, but originally it would have been just wide enough to take the teams of pack-ponies travelling the important bridleway running from Mitredale, over Irton Fell and by Hollow Moor, Skalderskew and Ponsonby, to Whitehaven. Very likely the smugglers used this route and the innocent looking hamlet of Nether Wasdale could have been an important meeting place for exchanging illicit cargoes. A relic of these bygone days was found by a labourer building a wall by the Irt in 1865. While removing stones from a cairn he discovered two blocks of pure plumbago (black lead) held together by a wooden pin. It was a beautifully engraved mould for making counterfeit coins in the reign of Edward IV or Richard III.

Thor started a fit of coughing as we climbed away from Nether Wasdale and I had to lead him for a while. By Bengarth Farm a swarm of flies drove themselves into a frenzy of excitement over the smell of horseflesh and I swept them off by the handful, smearing the ponies' necks with blood. They followed us in droves as we staggered along the road towards Gosforth and made life so unbearable we could hardly see where we were going. I had intended to join a bridleway above Gosforth and make for the remote farm of Skalderskew, but the flies were so troublesome and the heat so intense, it would have been cruel to prolong the discomfort of the ponies any further. With great reluctance I turned for Ravenglass.

We slithered down the soft tarmac of a steep hill into Gosforth and plodded drowsily past rows of cottages with little gardens full of sweet-scented flowers. By Gosforth Church I pulled the ponies under the shade of a clump of tall chestnut trees and, leaving them tied to a gate, I went into the churchyard to look at the famous Gosforth Cross, believed to be the tallest ancient cross in Britain. Standing about fourteen feet high and hewn out of a solid block of sandstone, the lower part is round and the upper part square and covered with the most beautifully intricate carvings on each face. The carvings are said to represent a Viking poem, telling of the struggle between good and evil.

All around the cross a mass of weathered headstones were spread about the green turf. Had all the victims of the great plague been laid to rest in this quiet corner, the grass would have had little room to grow for the village of Gosforth was particularly hard hit, with many families all but annihilated.

In the fourteenth century three strange happenings occurred throughout England. Cattle and oxen died suddenly after a short illness. At the same time fish were found dead in great numbers along the shores and birds fought so fiercely with each other thousands were killed and were strewn about the countryside. A chronicler of the time wrote 'All these wonders seem to have happened for the punishment of sinners or as an omen of things to come'. His latter prophecy was soon fulfilled when shortly afterwards a disastrous plague known everywhere as the Black Death, swept through the world and is said to have wiped out nine-tenths of the population of England. The Scots did not fare much better, having contracted the disease after a party of Border raiders had attacked Penrith on market day, killing many of the inhabitants and taking away spoil and prisoners. Almost one third of the population of Scotland was struck down as a result of the disease being carried over the border.

A fatal illness called 'sweating sickness' wreaked havoc among the dalesfolk of the Lake district and 'a deadly burning sweate so assailed their bodies and distempered their blood with a most ardent heat, that scarce one amongst a hundred did escape with life; for all in manner as soone as the sweate took them or within a short time after, yeilded the ghost'.

Markets were banned, but those whose living depended on selling their produce usually found a way round the law. The canny farmers around Keswick got the townsfolk to put their money in the beck, then they scooped it out and went away leaving the produce on the bank for the buyer to pick up.

For some strange reason the plague never entered the house of a tanner, tobacconist or shoemaker. Smoking was thought to help prevent the spread of the disease and children were made to smoke every day. A pupil at Eton College wrote that they were obliged to smoke in school every morning and that he was never whipped so much in his life as he was one morning for not smoking.

In one year the plague accounted for 172 of the population of the hamlet of Gosforth. How earnestly the inhabitants must have prayed, 'From lightning and tempest, from plague, pestilence and famine, from battle and murder and from sudden death, Good Lord deliver us'.

Leaving the churchyard we continued on through the main street, past the Midland Bank with all its unpleasant associations, and by Fleming Hall to join the old Whitehaven to Ravenglass coach road at Seascale Hall. In the days before the railway was built along the Cumberland coast a mail coach called the 'Princess Royal' and pulled by four horses, came every day from Ulverston to Whitehaven. Passengers were picked up at the various inns along the way and it is said that the coaches ran to a very strict time schedule. On Drigg Moor the ponies kicked up a cloud of choking red dust that settled over our sweat-soaked bodies and the heat was so great I had to stop every few hundred yards to rest the ponies in what shade the hedgerow could offer.

At the Victoria Hotel, by Drigg Railway Station, I enquired about the tide times for crossing the fords to Ravenglass and found I had two hours to wait before low water. At one time it was a favourite trick of landlords of inns close to the fords to give the wrong tide times so that unwitting travellers would have to wait for hours at the inn, or even stay the night. When the preacher, John Wesley, came this way in the middle of the eighteenth century, he was very indignant and wrote;

About eleven we were directed to a ford near Manchester Hall [obviously Waberthwaite ford and Muncaster Castle] which they said we might cross at noon. However, came thither they told us we could not cross, so we sat still till about one, when we then found we could have crossed at noon. However, we reached Whitehaven before night. But I have taken my leave of the sand road, especially as you have all the way to do with a generation of liars, who detain all strangers as long as they can, either for their own gain or their neighbours. I can advise no stranger to go this way.

I went out to slacken the girths and a kind lady from the station house appeared with two buckets of water. Thor drained his in one noisy gulp, but Jewel plunged her face right in as if to ease the pain of the hundreds of bites, then sipped slowly in between mouthfuls of grass torn from the verge. With the ponies cared for, I returned to the cool interior of the hotel, bought a glass of lager and a meat pie and sank into a corner with the barman's newspaper. Not having read a newspaper for weeks I was completely out of touch with events. I had not missed much. All over the world, manipulators of international politics were still playing their sinister chess game of pitting black against white, so that red could move into defence and force yellow to show its intentions. At home, those eloquent gentlemen elected by hopeful constituents were wasting valuable debating time hurling childish abuse at one another, beneath that ancient clock tower in London. On page three a well-endowed blonde thrust her voluptuous bosoms from a photograph and they looked so much like a pair of Jaffa grapefruits I was not sure whether she was showing them to me or offering them for sale. The rest of the paper was taken up with the bizarre world of various pop stars who, it seems, are unable to enjoy life without a daily dose of heroin. I returned the newspaper to the barman. The world had not improved while I had been away. The clock in the bar indicated that the fords would be passable, so I drained the last of the lager and went out into the sun.

Thor and Jewel stood in the shade of the station house,

enjoying a quiet doze, tails flicking automatically from side to side. Miraculously the flies had gone, except for an odd one or two who seemed to enjoy the game of landing on a rump, being catapulted off by a swishing tail and coming back for more. I returned the buckets to the lady, with my thanks, and climbed stiffly into the saddle for the last lap. The ponies picked their way carefully over the lines of the level crossing and then bounded forward with renewed energy, as if they knew they were close to home. The pace halted abruptly when they reached the wet mud at the edge of the ford. With the memory of Mosedale still fresh in their cautious heads, no amount of coaxing or cursing could persuade them to put more than an exploratory hoof into the ooze and they jumped back like a couple of springs. I had to get down off Thor and wade up to my knees across the ford before he plucked up courage to follow me and pull Jewel after him. Beyond the ford the coach road wended around the farm buildings of Hall Carleton and continued down to the beach at Saltcoats. The flat sand, recently abandoned by the receding tide, glistened like gold in the setting sun. At the water's edge flocks of black-headed gulls screeched and squabbled over lug worms and silver sprats trapped in isolated pools. Below the brightly painted cottages fish darted for safety as the ponies splashed through the ford that had once been part of the great highway along the coast of Cumberland. Many thousands of pack-horses and drovers had gone this way over the centuries, buying their goods at Ravenglass Fair and travelling the routes we had travelled, over the high passes, though fiercesome bogs and along the deep valleys, in rain, hail, snow and burning heat. The healthy growth of agriculture and commerce in the Lake District today is largely the result of those gallant men and their sturdy ponies. They were the lifelines of the dales and without them the sheep farmer would have perished and the local industries faded out of existence. For the past two months I had shared a little of their hardships and it had been an unforgettable experience.

As we rode down Ravenglass main street, I felt very sad. I had become accustomed to talking to the ponies and feeling their response and trust. I had driven them hard, lost my temper, cursed and shouted and got them into situations no pony should ever venture, yet they would always come to me when I called. They required nothing more than comfortable tack, a little food and a soft piece of ground to roll on. It was going to be very difficult to return to the tread-mill of everyday life and the inadequacies of the human race.

Dear old Thor and indestructible Jewel clattered over the cobbles into my yard and the journey was over.

A TOAST

To the feel of rough brown granite
And the acrid tang of soft brown peat;
To the ice-cold water of a mountain beck,
That quenches thirst and cools the aching feet;
To the smell of woodland paths and mountain pine,
Of heather, farmyards, sheep and wild thyme;
To the plaintive call of disturbed grouse,
The snow, the woolly mists, the wind, the driving rain;
To my good friends, Thor and Jewel,
And the day when we will roam again.

LONDON WALKS AND LEGENDS
by Mary Cathcart Borer

Walk down Holborn with Fagin and his partners-in-crime;
quench your thirst in the Hampstead pub where Dick Turpin
hung his hat; follow in the path of the death cart, which for
five centuries took its wretched cargo from Newgate prison to
the Tyburn gallows; visit old St Giles where Hogarth made his
grim study, Gin Lane; look down on London with the young
apprentice Dick Whittington's eyes ...

London is one of the world's oldest and most beautiful cities.
More than this, it is richly endowed with literature, history and
legend. The rhymes 'London Bridge' and 'Oranges and Lemons'
have rung down the centuries in children's singing games and
are known to all. But what are their historical origins in Old
London? Mary Cathcart Borer answers this and many other
fascinating questions as she guides the reader on a series of
short and immensely rewarding walks around the city. It is an
absorbing glimpse into London's rich, dark and imaginative
past.

ILLUSTRATED

£1.25

WEST COUNTRY WALKS AND LEGENDS
by J H N Mason

Here Tristan and Iseult forswore their love before the King ...

St Nectan's legendary treasure lies hidden beneath a
waterfall ...

And the ghostly presence of King Arthur haunts his legendary
birthplace, Tintagel.

This book is for the visitor to the West Country who wants to
see the best of its varied scenery and at the same time learn
something of the region's rich heritage. Mr Mason has selected
the most fascinating legends of Cornwall, Devon, Dorset and
Somerset, and in each case gives full details of how to reach
their location and the best way to explore the area on foot.
Most of the walks are short and easy, suitable for taking
children along – a few are longer to suit the more energetic.

ILLUSTRATED

£1.25

TITLES AVAILABLE IN THE WALKS AND LEGENDS SERIES PUBLISHED BY GRANADA PAPERBACKS

Lakeland Walks and Legends	
by Brain J Bailey	£1.50 ☐
London Walks and Legends	
by Mary Cathcart Borer	£1.25 ☐
West Country Walks and Legends	
by J H N Mason	£1.25 ☐
Welsh Walks and Legends	
by Showell Styles	£1.00 ☐
Scottish Walks and Legends Volume 1	
by Janice Anderson and Edmund Swinglehurst	£1.50 ☐
Scottish Walks and Legends Volume 2	
by Janice Anderson and Edmund Swinglehurst	£1.50 ☐

All these books are available at your local bookshop or newsagent, or can be ordered direct from the publisher. Just tick the titles you want and fill in the form below.

Name ....

Address ....

....

Write to Granada Cash Sales, PO Box 11, Falmouth, Cornwall TR10 9EN

Please enclose remittance to the value of the cover price plus:

UK: 40p for the first book, 18p for the second book plus 13p per copy for each additional book ordered to a maximum charge of £1.49.

BFPO and EIRE: 40p for the first book, 18p for the second book plus 13p per copy for the next 7 books, thereafter 7p per book.

OVERSEAS: 60p for the first book and 18p for each additional book.

Granada Publishing reserve the right to show new retail prices on covers, which may differ from those previously advertised in the text or elsewhere.